Christian Mysticism
A Psychotheology

Christian Mysticism
A Psychotheology

by
William McNamara, O.C.D.
Spiritual Life Institute
Nova Nada
N. Kemptville, Yarmouth Co., Nova Scotia

Franciscan Herald Press
Chicago, Illinois 60609

Copyright © 1981
Franciscan Herald Press
1434 West 51st Street
Chicago, Illinois 60609

The author acknowledges with gratitude the permission
of the following publishers to use copyrighted material:
Andrews and McMeel, Inc., *Sin, Liberty and Law*, by
Louis Monden, S.J., copyright 1965 by Sheed and Ward,
Inc.; Dodd, Mead, and Company, Inc., *Orthodoxy*, by
Gilbert Keith Chesterton, copyright 1908, by Dodd,
Mead and Company, Inc.; copyright renewed 1935 by G.
K. Chesterton; the Seabury Press, *Body as Spirit*,
by Charles Davis, copyright 1976 by the Seabury Press,
Inc.

Library of Congress Cataloging in Publication Data

McNamara, William.
 Christian mysticism.

 1. Mysticism. 2. Mysticism—Psychology.
I. Title.
BV5082.M25   248.2'2   80-13193
ISBN 0-8199-0793-6

Published with Ecclesiastical Permission
MADE IN THE UNITED STATES OF AMERICA

Contents

To
All those I have
loved and lost—
with compunction

Preface

"Man is born beyond psychology and he dies beyond
it, but he can live beyond it only through vital experience of his own."

Otto Rank, *Beyond Psychology*

This is not a psychological textbook or a scientific investigation
of psychological or mystical "cases" but an attempt to answer
some essential questions: What is mysticism? contemplation?
mystical experience? Is mysticism for everyone or only a select
few? Is it a special kind of experience or an experience more
familiar to us all? How do we enter and persevere along the
mystic way and reach the end? What constitutes a good environment for the mystical life? What threatens it? How does mystical experience relate to reason, affectivity, the body, liturgy,
doctrine, Scripture, the Church?

This is a practical psychotheological book without psychological jargon which zeroes in on the simplest and truest way for
people in the West to become mystics: by immersion in the In-
carnational worldliness of the *Christian Way*. It appeals
passionately to every reader to risk everything for a vital experience of his own.

I am grateful to the Spiritual Life Institute's quarterly
magazine, *Desert Call*, where some of this material first appeared, and especially indebted to Tessa Bielecki for her outstanding editing of the original manuscript. Once again I thank

my Nova Nada community for the support, sacrifice, and hard work that made this book possible.

William McNamara O.C.D.
Pentecost Sunday, 1977

Introduction

Part I: Imprisonment

1. The Mystical Vocation

The mystic is not a special kind of person, but everyone is—or ought to be—a special kind of mystic.

What Is Mysticism?—We need to eliminate some of the misunderstandings that surround the word "mysticism." Mysticism is not "tripping out" but "standing in." It is no pain-killer and does not remove us from the anguish of conflict and doubt, the chaos, flesh and blood of the world. The mystic is not a spooky introvert, prowling around in the sanctuary of his own soul. He is deeply and profoundly immersed in the world.

The mystic doesn't just do something; he stands there, seeing everything all at once against the background of eternity. Mysticism is more readily caught than taught. The only valid apostolate is the sharing of mystical contemplation, our own experiential awareness of God.

Western Mysticism—Mystical life on earth reached its zenith in Christ and remains at its peak, available to us through the religious traditions, rituals and scriptures of the West. Whether divine union is experienced depends partly on environment, preeminently on psychophysical constitution. The transparent personality is more easily recognized as mystical.

Phony mysticism abounds because we copy the outer behavior of genuine mystics without any grasp of their inner Godward dispositions. The mystic *feels* the presence of God. Affectivity and rationality are not opposed. We believe only what we have conceived in the whole body, not merely the brain.

The Code-Cult Connection—Mystical *life* is the same as mystical *experience* (singular) but not the same as mystical *experiences* (plural). The core of religion is not a pure, unmediated inward affair but includes liturgical and devotional activities as well as apostolic endeavors. Mysticism, dogma and the ecclesiastical institution exist in a state of tension but also in vital unity.

Mystical experience is not the fruit of a direct and systematic effort but is a gratuitous gift of God. The aim of mystical contemplation is love.

America's Spiritual Crisis—The mystic must not be confused with the psychic. We are presently witnessing a psychical revolution that has won the approval of science. There is little evidence, however, of any mystical revolution.

Our human predicament may be described as a mystical or spiritual crisis, a crisis in contemplation. Man's natural mystical powers are seriously atrophied and must be reactivated. Activity without contemplation is blind. We are fed and sustained by a mystical theology, amused and confused by any other.

2. Our Rational Prison

What is it that kills contemplation and makes the passionate life of Christian mysticism so difficult to enjoy? The causes are multiple and complex. But there does seem to be a matrix, which I would designate as rationalism.

The Rational Bulldozer—We try insanely to bulldoze our way rationally into the secret of being, ruthlessly tearing the world to shreds in our frantic effort to label everything in tidy categories that fit into our prefabricated logical framework.

Mysticism keeps man sane. As long as you have mystery you have health. There is no way to package mystery into a collection of verbalized concepts.

Man has been reduced to a mind machine. The substitution of mental concepts for living experience keeps the exigencies of life at a safe distance. We must risk the security and certainty of a theory of existence carefully concocted in our heads and suffer our way into a rich and rewarding experience of life.

Our contemporary preoccupation with knowledge as possession leaves us dying from lack of communion.

The problem of evil helps us out of our rational imprisonment by being a strict logical self-contradiction. It interrupts our relatively abstract approach to God and introduces us to the existential response to pain, suffering, and absurdity: passion-in-the-face-of-paradox.

Machiavellian Madness—The quintessence of rationalism is Machiavellianism, which takes its name from Niccolò Machiavelli, the sixteenth-century Italian statesman-author who wrote *The Prince*. Machiavelli insists it is better to rely on force and be feared rather than be loved. Cruelty is better in the long run because it works. Power becomes an end in itself as persons and policies are reduced to means. Machiavellianism has become more than a political affair. It is now a pervasive factor influencing and shaping all human relationships.

Machiavellianism nurtures the seeds of violence by turning man into a means for the attainment of an end outside of man. Reason balks at man as an end because the mystery of man cannot be ransacked. According to Machiavelli, the end justifies the means; and man is a means. But he will always leave a residue: suffering, an infallible sign of sacredness. Man should not suffer from being a means; he should suffer from not being an end.

The ascetical-mystical life is the redirection of vitality inhumanly dissipated in the use of man as a means.

Part II: Liberation

3. Soul-Friending

Theologians and psychologists of the spiritual life have always agreed upon the necessity of spiritual direction.

The Value of Personal Direction—Personal direction does not produce mystical experience but prepares us for it. A lack of spiritual growth may be attributed to the absence of spiritual direction. If spiritual direction were no more than a curb to self-will, it would be invaluable. "Who constitutes himself his own master becomes the disciple of a fool."

The clumsy title "spiritual director" seems almost entirely unsatisfactory. "Soul-friend" is more appropriate. There can be nothing casual or careless about the relationship between two "friends" involved in "soul-care."

Finding a Soul-Friend—We should choose our soul-friend with care, governed by reason and faith, not merely our natural inclination. We should look for five qualities in him: personal prayer and holiness, reverence for the mystery of the human person, prudence, experience and learning.

The soul-friend must cope continually with the demands of God and human weakness. He is nothing but an instrument in the hands of God. God alone can deify. The soul-friend is only a servant.

Soul-Care—The soul-friend helps us avoid the common mistakes and the typical pitfalls of the spiritual life: pride, delusion, hyper-introspection, quietism, fanaticism, fixation, presumption, "strong-man" asceticism, and preoccupation with the psychophysical phenomena that sometimes occur during certain phases of the mystical life.

One of the most valuable services he offers is in the vastly important area of prayer. He can be particularly helpful during the transitional period when God moves the soul from meditation to mystical contemplation. This "dark night of the soul" occurs not only in our prayer life but in other areas of our life as well, when we suffer from confusion, incapacity, and an overpowering sense of our own nothingness.

4. The Experience of Nada

Nada is Spanish for nothing. The experience of nothingness lies at the heart of the whole spiritual life. It is the beginning of the mystical journey.

The Sense of Nothingness—We need not be afraid of nothing. We cannot have something without nothing. "To be or not to be" is *not* the question. The inescapable sense of nothingness is as positive as the sense of reality, as personal as the sense of self. My sense of nothingness depends on my sense of being. The sense of nothingness becomes most salubrious when ultimate being is recognized as God. If we are not comparably impressed with the divine love and mercy, we can be thrust relentlessly into despair. There is within us a concept of perfect being. Nothing on this earth completely satisfies us. We cannot rest until we rest in God.

Nothingness is not only the exclusive entrance into the mystic way; it is the only door into mental health and moral freedom. It is therefore regrettable that neither Freud nor Jung opened this door. Both Freud and Jung got stuck in the empirical standpoint. Christ himself is the psychologist par excellence.

The Denial of Death—Insight into our own nothingness prepares us for death. Until we face death and embrace its terror, life escapes us. At the heart of our psychopathological tendencies and our defense mechanisms lies not sexual repression but life-failure. Our anxiety is due to the devastating demands of life, with death lurking in the shadows, leering out at us from the heart of every life situation.

We've got to die and be reborn long before we leave a corpse behind us. Rebirth is an excruciatingly painful all-or-nothing process as thick layers of our neurotic shield peel off and expose our pulsating vitality to the awe-ful dread of truth.

Death must involve a kind of violence if our proud self-imprisonment is to be broken open. The mystic prepares for the final act of death by striking mortal blows to his false self. Through his poverty, chastity, and obedience (no fuss, no lust, no rust) he embraces death daily and draws from that confrontation radical consequences for life really lived.

The Nothingness Neurosis—Whenever we deny our death and repress our sense of nothingness, we are plagued by "the nothing-

ness neurosis." If we are deprived of meaning, we are thrust
into an intolerable form of life-failure.

Our big problem is the meaninglessness and boredom of
human life, the strange human incapacity to lay hold of experience. Boredom cripples the will. If the will lies dormant for
long periods of time, life fails. When life drags on, the will runs
down. Increased effort of will leads to an increased sense of
meaning which sharpens our appetite for life.

Most of us let the robot take over most of the time, leaving
us in a state of psychic numbness. There is something wrong
with normal human consciousness. Our sense of values only
comes alive in moments of great excitement or crisis. The mentally healthy individual lives under such divine inner pressure—
not nervous tension—that he is always tapping deep levels of
vital reserves and enjoying mystical vision.

Part III: Celebration

5. Christian Vitality

When we live in Christ we know what mysticism is. We are
graced with such amazing vitality that we enjoy realized union
with God.

Awakened in Faith—Faith is the only proximate and immediate
means of union with God. To live by faith is to go in one direction. To be without faith is to act convulsively. Faith is rooted in
the deepest domain of man far below the range of the senses.
The world is divided into those who are asleep, living apathetically in the shallows, and those who are awake and enlivened by
faith.

The Celebration of Life—All man needs to survive is a little
bread and water. But in order to enjoy real Christian vitality, he
needs to celebrate the gift of his life and the whole of creation
that makes life so liveable. Most of us do not know how to celebrate because we don't know what it feels like to be alive. In the

name of safety and sanity we discourage the primitive activity characteristic of childhood and essential to full human life.

The Meaning of Festivity—Festivity is more than the absence of work, and leisure more than our free time. When we celebrate we imitate God who stopped work on the Seventh Day, contemplated his world, and took delight in it. Joy, the fruit of festivity, is pure gift and cannot be induced. It is the echo of God's presense. No man can live without pleasure. But a sham production is worse than no festivity at all. There can be no true celebration without sacrifice, no feast without a prior fast.

Biblical Sensuousness—Our inability to celebrate life with reckless abandon may be due in part to our traditional suspicion of the body. There is a difference between sensuousness and sensuality. Mystical life, a total human response to mystery, is necessarily sensuous. Sensuality, in some respects, is the enslavement of the body to the domineering consciousness of a mind alienated from its bodiliness. The traditional version had it the other way around.

Sin makes holy sensuousness difficult, not because the body is unruly but because the mind is twisted. Freeing ourselves from sin is worth all the trouble. What begins as a necessary discipline becomes a holy act of reverence.

Freedom—We are afraid to be free, to live out our responseability. Who wants to be vulnerable? The irresponsible busybody may have life, but he has no spirit and therefore cannot transfigure matter.

Spontaneity and universal kinship are the hallmarks of a free man. But universal love is killed regularly by an awesome trio: time, space, and numbers. The inability to keep love alive is the most culpable human crime.

Christ came to free us from everything but himself.

6. Our Daily Bread

Man is what he eats. The Biblical account of God's passion for man is a sensuous piece of literature that presents man as a hungry being and the world as his food.

Bread and Wine—The Eucharistic celebration is a concentrate of the overall life-experience of God's presence in all things. We misconstrue the meaning and misuse the sacrament when by religious pronouncements of faith we try to switch the profane into the sacred and wrest God from above.

Sacraments are tools of denuminization, making available and bearable the dazzling dimension of the Holy Other. Jesus didn't institute a sacrament of the Eucharist. He entered into the sacramentality of the universe.

"Not by Bread Alone"—Eating and drinking the Word of God is a concept that runs through the whole Bible. Spiritual reading is a way of feeding the mind on a mind richer than our own, a sure test of our mind's wellbeing.

We must read seriously, regularly, and discriminately. It is spiritual suicide to fill the mind with junk. We can only afford to read the best.

Spiritual reading "traps" us into praying and serves as a hallway into meditation.

Biblical Humor—If some of us find Scripture tasteless reading, perhaps we do not understand its humorous style. We often misunderstand the Bible by an interpretation that is too solemn and sober. The Bible is not a series of straight assertions but a collection of puns and witticisms. Puns enrich meanings. Wit explodes them.

To understand literally is one thing, to understand psychologically is another. Christ—the complete humorist—transformed literal into psychological meaning.

A Cry of the Heart—Unless we feel that we are nothing, prayer is useless. The Christian at prayer does not always sit in a serene and tranquil posture of stillness and receptivity. Sometimes he pounds his fists on the wall or paces the floor. Whenever he enters into prayer he assumes he may not come out alive.

No prayer is answered unless it is in accord with the Lord's Prayer.

Prayer is a cry of the heart. It must be passionate and grow out of our own inner truth. Rooting prayer in the real precludes pious piffle.

The Our Father is "the prayer of the heart" par excellence. This may impress you more profoundly if you meditate on it backwards.

Part I: Imprisonment

Chapter 1
The Mystical Vocation

The mystic is not a special kind of person, but everyone is—or ought to be—a special kind of mystic. Mysticism is nothing esoteric. It is not the privilege of a few but an experience every one of us should know first hand.

What is Mysticism?

Mysticism is infinitely too subjective to teach. It is more readily caught than taught. For example, the supreme objective of the Spiritual Life Institute, founded in the desert of Sedona, Arizona, and the woods of Kemptville, Nova Scotia, is to foster the spirit of mystical contemplation in our North American culture so that our political, social, economic and domestic existence is inspired by it. And yet the Institute wouldn't dare try to teach mysticism. All we can do, and all we plan to do, as we grow and develop, is to set the stage as humanly as possible for the mystical experience.

When man becomes as human as he can become, then he is properly and thoroughly divinized so that he thinks and loves like God, and mystical life is inevitable. I made this clear in my earlier works, *The Art of Being Human* and *The Human Adventure*. In these two efforts, I used the term "contemplation" rather than mysticism. In *Mystical Passion* and again in this current

3

volume, I prefer the term "mysticism," although contemplation and mysticism are essentially the same. It is crucial, however, to eliminate many of the misunderstandings and misconceptions that surround the meaning of both these words.

Though you cannot teach mysticism, or explain it adequately, or superficially decide to achieve it, you must know as much about it as you can theoretically and do as much about it as you can, practically, in order to become mystical. You need to know what mysticism is not.

What we are discussing here is nothing like the false mysticism of mass society or any fanatical movement which whips up collective enthusiasm or party loyalty and easily captivates the contemporary man uprooted from the universe and out of touch with his own depths. There are many other escapes from the empirical, external self which might seem to be but are not mysticism. Mysticism is not what drug enthusiasts call "tripping out." It is more like "standing in," alert and alive, with the highest possible focus of human attention on the present moment. It is standing willfully and deliberately in awe and wonder before the unveiled mystery of reality.

Mysticism is not a pain-killer. It provides no escape from the world but puts us in touch with the world. The mystic is not a rigid, unbending, unworldly man. He is in love with God, with life, and is therefore supple, tolerant and flexible.

Mysticism is not a way out of anguish, conflict and doubt. On the contrary—the deep, inexpressible certitude of the mystical experience awakens a tragic anguish and opens many questions in the depths of the heart, like wounds that cannot stop bleeding. Mystics often suffer more than anyone else because they are so sympathetic and compassionate. They may harbor the gravest doubts because their childish puerile faith, the spurious faith of their everyday life, explodes before them. A veritable bonfire burns to ashes their old, worn-out words, clichés and slogans. Even their most holy conceptions and sacred ideas of God are consumed in the fire of this great holocaust.

The mystic discovers through his contemplation, his personal encounter with the living God, that he knows nothing about God. He knows not what but only *that* God is. He learns that God is no thing (nothing, *nada*), no what, but a pure Who. God is the Thou before whom the mystic's inmost I springs into awareness. God is the "I am" before whom the mystic echoes his own "I am." The mystic stands defenselessly, helplessly, and humbled before God's holy scrutiny. Mysticism is not a trance, an ecstasy or an enthusiasm. It is not the wild frenzy of religious exultation. It is not the imagination of lights or the hearing of unutterable words. These do not emanate from the deep self but from the somatic unconscious. They are an overflow of the dionysian forces within us which may happen in conjunction with a religious experience but do not contitute mysticism.

Mysticism is not the affair of a quiet and passive temperament which naturally loves to sit and do nothing. The mystic is not a spooky introvert, an isolated thinker who simply loves to ruminate or reflect, prowling around in the sanctuary of his own psyche. Most of the mystics I know are strong, robust and vibrant, almost fierce, obsessed with a Zorba-like, or better, Christ-like madness.

The true mystic does not merely explore his own consciousness but savors the Real. He is not a rigid, unbending, unworldly man, aloof from flesh and blood, the turmoil, chaos and pleasures of the world. Some of the most mystical people are deeply and profoundly immersed in the world, thoroughly engaged in political and social life, rearing dozens of children. They are great lovers and great fighters. They are mystical simply because they are basically and essentially great lovers of God and his whole creation. Some of my favorite mystics are prophets like John the Baptist and Elijah, saintly women like Joan of Arc and Elizabeth of Hungary, disciplined, wild men like Zorba the Greek, Holden Caulfield, or Mr. Blue. These great mystics are not indifferent but deeply in love with the world. Their love of the world does not diminish but enhances their dynamic, irresistible and burning love of God. It is possible for a man to become totally detached in everything and unattached to God. But he is not a saint; he's a stuffed shirt. He is not all aglow with the Spirit, consumed with the fire of God's love, but simply "into" piety.

Mysticism is not inward torpor. It is a magnetic, mobilizing peace characterized by the wise passiveness of St. John of the Cross: "I abandoned and forgot myself . . . leaving my cares forgotten among the lilies." It is the highest form of action. The mystic doesn't just do something; he stands there. He doesn't even take a pole with him when he goes fishing because he has no need to justify doing nothing. Being compels him to do nothing. When God speaks, the mystic must do nothing but listen; when God appears he must simply behold; when God gives he must do nothing but receive. Responding to God's initiative this way distinguishes this positive and gracious quiet from the error of quietism, the limp passivity of the sluggard often confused with the alert stillness of the spiritual athlete. English mystic and theologian Walter Hilton describes the paradoxical activity of such peace: "This restful travail is far from fleshly idleness and from blind security. It is full of ghostly work, but it is called rest . . . an holy idleness and a rest most busy."

Having cleared away some of the outstanding debris, we are in a better position to say something more positive about mysticism.

Mystical contemplation is the experiential grasp of reality as subjective. Not mine—that would pertain to the external, superficial self—but as myself in existential mystery. Mysticism does not meet reality through a process of deduction but through an intuitive awakening in which our free and personal reality becomes fully alive in its own existential depths which open out into the mystery of God. If we can discover ourselves in depth, we discover God and simultaneously discover Christ. We can almost say there is an identity between my most real, profound, and transcendent self and the real Christ.

If I am a mystic, I have come into ownership of myself. I have achieved through asceticism and discipline and the controlled wildness of love, the mastery of my own human instrument. Only when I have achieved ownership of myself may I give myself to the world and enter into the sharing of the contemplation I enjoy—which is the only valid definition of the apostolate. If my apostolate is not simply a sharing of my mystical contemplation, my own experiential awareness of God, then it is phony, noisy and absurd.

No one can proclaim the contemplation of Christ and the Church in an effective and lasting way, unless he himself participates in it. How can we proclaim or spread abroad by activity, however zealous, what we do not know ourselves in a personal, experiential way?

"The most important thing to do is to be," said Lao-tzu. Apostles are not self-appointed but sent by God, after he has touched and transformed them. Such men are rare. When they show up they always seem to be men of prayer; silent and solitary men, God-filled, God-intoxicated, not saying much, not doing much, but keeping God's love alive and his presence felt in a world full of half-hearted, talkative, busy men who live frightened, fragmented "lives of quiet desperation."

To engage in the natural art of contemplation is to look long and steadily, leisurely and lovingly at any thing—a tree, a child, a pear, a kitten, a hippopotamus, and really "see" the whole of it; not to steal an idea of it, but to know it by experience, a pure intuition born of love. This is not an aggressive act but gratuitous. Being discloses its hidden secrets as we look, wait, wonder, and stand in awe of it—not inquisitively but receptively. The mystic—that is, the contemplative—is never utilitarian or Machiavellian, greedily trying to get something out of everything. He simply stands before being, before the world, before the universe, before another human being, a plant, an animal. He enjoys it and leaves himself wide open to its revelation, to its disclosures of mystery, of truth, of love.

Mystical contemplation is more than a consideration of

abstract truths about God, more than meditation on what we believe. Mysticism is an awakening enlightenment, an intuitive grasp whereby love is sure of God's creative and dynamic intervention in our concrete, commonplace, daily life. Hence the mystic does not simply find a clear idea of God and confine him within the limits of that idea and hold him there as a prisoner. No, the mystic is carried away by God into his own realm, his own mystery and his own freedom. Mysticism is a pure and virginal knowledge, poor in concepts, poorer still in reasoning, but able by its very poverty and purity to follow the Word wherever he may go.

Mysticism is man's long, loving look at reality to which he is united by love. It is the highest expression of man's intellectual and spiritual life. Its activity is its own end. Mysticism has no utilitarian purposes: just looking, loving, being utterly, magnificently, wildly useless. It is life itself fully awake and active and aware that it is alive. Mysticism is awe and wonder at the sacredness of life and of being and of the invisible, transcendent and infinite abundant source of being. It knows the source obscurely, inexplicably, but with a certitude beyond reason. It is a veritable vision of the Godhead—in the human, earthy context. This act by which man sees who he is—not in isolation, but against the background of eternity—and so simultaneously and experientially sees who God is—this is genuine mysticism.

Western Mysticism

Mystical life is both the most normal and the highest expression of the spiritual life. It involves the highest levels of participation in the intimate, trinitarian lovelife of the Godhead. This loving involvement with Ultimate Being issues in the deification of man. God is the primary source and active agent of this divine transformation. Man is the recipient of divine disclosures and becomes a mystic by being drawn by grace into the ineffable mystery.

Mystical life on earth reached its zenith in Christ and remains at its peak, available to us through the religious traditions, rituals, and scriptures of the West. No one can afford to neglect the wisdom of the East. But a Westerner ought to be rooted and steeped in his own tradition, which contains the richest store of mysticism in the world. It is this Christian mysticism that concerns us here.

Whether mystical union is experienced depends partly on our environment, particularly our beliefs, but preeminently on our psychophysical constitution. This accounts for the fact, otherwise inexplicable, that mystical experience like artistic creation or scientific intelligence, is often shared by members of the same family: for example, St. John of the Cross, and his brother.

Not everyone is mystical to the same degree. Some individuals are more easily recognizable as mystics. There is a psychological factor that identifies and distinguishes them from the grace-full spiritual man who is not usually considered a mystic. The felicity and frequency with which the mystic consciously experiences divine union depends upon his particular temperament.

E.I. Watkins, born in 1888, my favorite living philosopher, has explained this in terms of the transparent or opaque personality. The latter, for instance, sees the same comedy as the former but never laughs; hears the same music but never moves a muscle; suffers the same embarrassment but never turns red. The inner experiences of the transparent personality, however, always register on his countenance or in his external behavior. What happens in his spiritual depths, at the center of his soul, rises easily to the conscious surface. What occurs in the deep recesses of the opaque personality will seldom, if ever, become apparent. Transparent personalities are much more likely to translate an inner experience into a painting, a song, or a poem.

Both the transparent and the opaque person are in union with God, but only the transparent one becomes conscious of it. Both are drawn by God into the deepest dimensions of the human adventure, the mystical depths of the spiritual life, but only the transparent personality exhibits mystical experiences. The opaque personality, though raised by God into the mystical existence of God-manhood, does not show it or even know it. Despite this, he may be just as holy as his transparent counterpart. Theologically speaking, both types are mystics; but phenomenally speaking, only the transparent person is, because he experiences God's active presence within him and is, obviously, recognizably mystical.

Unfortunately, because of all of our monkey business, phony mysticism abounds. Like monkeys, people copy the outer behavior of genuine mystics without any grasp of their inner Godward dispositions. It's what's inside that counts. I remember Alan Watts comparing a mystic to a musical genius. Strictly speaking, a composer is inspired when melody emerges from the depths of his mind. To convey that melody to others he writes it down on paper, employing a technical knowledge which enables him to name the notes he heard in his mind.

This fact is important: his technical knowledge does not create the tune in his mind; it simply provides him with a complicated alphabet, and is no more the source of music than the literary alphabet and the rules of grammar are the sources of men's ideas. What music teachers call "rules" of harmony are simply observations on the harmonies most usually used by such people as Mozart and Beethoven. Mozart and Beethoven did not use them because they were the rules but because they liked their sound. It is necessary for a composer to study harmony in order to identify the chords which he hears in his mind, but he does not use his knowledge to construct chords unless he is a mere imitator of other people. In the same way, language is used not to create thoughts but to express them, and mastery of prose does not make a great thinker.

The spiritual genius—the mystic—works the same way as the musical genius. He has a wider scope because his technique of expression, his alphabet, is every possible human activity. Amid all mystics, some more than others, *the presence of God is felt.* The mystic expresses this feeling two ways: first, by living a certain kind of life; and, secondly, by translating his or her feeling into thoughts and words.

People who have not had this feeling observe his actions and words, and from them formulate the "rules" of religious morality and theology. There are bound to be distortions. It is strange how foreign any original and unique religious feeling is to the average human being, even to the professional religious personality. The essential thing about the mystic is his feeling, not his ideas and actions, for these are only reflections of the feeling, and a reflection existing without light is a sham. Therefore just as great technical proficiency will not make a creative genius in music, so morality, theology, and discipline will not make a genius in religion, for these are the results of religious experience, not the causes, and by themselves can no more produce it than the tail can be made to wag the dog.

As we shall see in the next chapter, on "Our Rational Prison," our rational society repudiates feeling as the human response to reality. Feeling is larger and livelier than emotion and is much more readily assimilated by an honest-to-goodness, down-to-earth intellectual life. Unfortunately feeling and emotion are often treated as synonyms. Emotion directly refers to bodily agitation. Feeling includes emotion as a bodily component but refers, not to the organic reverberations of our affective life, but to our affective responses understood as conscious, insightful responses to intelligently grasped situations. When we speak of feeling, we imply an element of rational appreciation of what is felt. Knowledge of this factual experience should preclude any fatuous forms of anti-intellectual rebellion against the real enemy—rationalism, or what that enemy has thrust us into: a science-based, sensate culture of industrialism. Affectivity and rationality are not opposed. Genuine affective responses are rational.

The nature of religious feeling is explored and explained superbly in a 1976 book entitled *Body as Spirit* by Charles Davis, now on the faculty of St. Michael's College at the University of Toronto. For an elucidation of this central but tricky subject I can do no better than to lean heavily on Davis' treatment. He asserts that feeling is a cognitive process; but it is also much more than that. To that effect, he quotes William Butler Yeats: "We only believe those thoughts which have been conceived not in the brain but in the whole body."

A merely intellectual response to reality is not enough. It is a restricted response, engaging neither the total self nor the total reality of the object, whereas feeling refers to a total response, actuating what we are as persons. As Davis says: "The appropriate distinction needed to locate feeling precisely is not between intelligence and affectivity but between the spontaneous connatural response of the subject to reality as object and the subsequent appropriation and formulation of that response in conceptualization and judgment."[1]

The Code-Cult Connection

Mystical *life* is the same as mystical *experience* (singular) but not the same as mystical *experiences* (plural). Whereas mystical *life* is indispensable for the attainment of eminent holiness and consists in an intimate and sacrificial union of the will with God, the union which is charity, mystical *experiences* are not. Although secondary mystical phenomena may be helpful, they are nonessential, transitory and fraught with danger. (See Chapter III, section on "Soul-Care," pages 49–73).

Davis has convinced me to distinguish between religious experience and religious feeling. Religious experience refers in a comprehensive sense to all the activities and passivities, as long as they are genuine and sincere, that we call religious. This includes myth, symbol, ritual, mystical practices, doctrinal beliefs and practical, social and institutional activity, as well as the inner events of religious consciousness. The inclusion of all this highlights the fact that the core of religion is not a pure, unmediated inward affair. Liturgical and devotional activities as well as apostolic endeavors, plus all the virtue exercised in life and death situations, should be included in religious experience. Yet most descriptive or philosophic works on mystical experience still depend on a line of thought which has identified mystical experience with a religious experience conceived in a subjective and emotional fashion, entirely distinct and separate from code and cult.

All Christian mystics have been deeply indebted to revelation for their experience. The typical spirit of them all is summed up by St. John of the Cross when he says:

> In order to say a little about this dark night, I shall trust neither to experience nor to knowledge, since both may fail and deceive; but, while not omitting to make such use as I can of these two things, I shall avail myself, in all that, with the Divine favour, I have to say, or, at the least, in that which is most important and dark to the understanding, of Divine Scripture; for, if we guide ourselves by this, we shall be unable to stray, since He Who speaks therein is the Holy Spirit.[2]

Christian mysticism is inseparable from the Bible. The doctrine of St. John the Evangelist and St. Paul not only furnishes the basis of Christian mysticism, but constitutes the most authentic realization of it. St. John's theology of God as Love, Light, and Spirit, and salvation as the new birth in water and the Spirit, carrying with it an unshakable certitude, is indubitably mystical. John's Gospel has always been known as the "spiritual" Gospel: it contains all the great words of mysticism.

St. Paul, to whom God reveals himself directly, and who preaches a mystery into which one is initiated by a knowledge, a grace and a love, all works of an interior God, is no less mystical. Though he tries to write soberly of the profound psychical changes which came to him, and of the heavenly manifestations he enjoyed, he cannot restrain his pen, and he communicates something of his own rapture as he attempts to relate what never can be told. His writings are a treasure house of mystical doctrine.

Later mysticism will deviate at times by forgetting the characteristics of New Testament mysticism. But there in Sacred Writ the historic character of revelation and the Incarnation, the importance of objective mysticism (i.e., the symbolic role of visible reality), and the necessity of liturgy are not forgotten.

It is perilous to dissociate Christian mystics from the doctrine which nourishes them and from the Church which sustains them. Obviously doctrine plays more than a secondary role in the experience of St. Augustine, St. Bonaventure, St. Bernard, Johannes Tauler, Blessed Henry Suso, and Blessed John Ruysbroeck. They are typical of all the Christian mystics who also loved the liturgy, especially the Mass, and participated in it fully unto the end. St. John of the Cross was so completely and delicately in tune with the liturgical year that one of his confreres claimed that they could tell what liturgical feast or season they were celebrating by looking at the saint. This is not surprising since, as Pope St. Pius X said, "The liturgy is the primary and indispensable source of the true Christian spirit."

Historians and psychologists tend to reduce mystical experience to a psychological phenomenon without object or foundation. So do many Protestant theologians who are worried about losing the historical realities of salvation in Hellenistic speculation. Whence arises the celebrated but unacceptable opposition between mystical and prophetic piety, between neo-Platonic mysticism and Biblical faith, developed by Nathan Söderblom, Friedrich Heiler, Karl Barth, Emil Brunner, and Oscar Cullmann.

No one in his exposition, and apparently also in his life, preserves and cultivates the unity of mysticism, dogma and the ecclesiastical institution better than Baron Friedrich Von Hügel, a twentieth-century Englishman. In his classic contribution, *The Mystical Element of Religion,* Von Hügel says religion is built only with the aid of a mystical élan, a doctrinal speculation, and a communitarian institution which subsist in it as varied elements in a state of tension, but also in vital unity. To suppress one of the elements amounts to abolishing religion in its richest meaning.

The mystical element of religion is constituted by an ontological presence and an active infusion of Infinite Spirit into finite spirit. The fragile creature becomes acutely aware of his contingence and finitude, and although his first inclination is to withdraw from the divine pressure at the core of his being, he finally capitulates and hurls himself into the infinite abyss, into the ground of his being, into the pure, naked being of the All. But mysticism is never "pure" in the sense that it drives out and replaces the institutional and intellectual dimensions of religion. The genuine mystic, however solitary and exalted, has a profound impact on the contingent world, historical events, and the social community.

The reader of Von Hügel needs to be somewhat cautious, however, in one area: the sense of contingency and finiteness is not, of itself, a mystical experience, an immediate experience of the spirit. It may take a long time, many years perhaps, for this spark to become a fire. In fact, as we shall see soon enough, the tragic sense of our own nothingness can be, and often is, pre-religious, and is open to many directions.

It is important to note that all Catholic theologians agree that mystical experience is not a simple psychological phenomenon; it is always trans-psychological, because it is in ontological continuity with supernatural realities. But the ontological continuity in no way prevents psychological discontinuity. This means that the primary characteristic of what St. John of the Cross calls the "mystical intelligence" is the experiential manner or the new psychological mode of its apprehension.

It is God whom mystical knowledge perceives immediately and experientially in the historic revelation of Christ, the sacramental life, and the ecclesiastical organism. It is not contradictory to unite indissolubly the immediacy of mystical knowledge to all the Christian mediations.

When the mystics try to describe their intimate encounter with ultimate reality, with God himself at the core or apex of their being, they speak of a simultaneous experience of night and light. Why is this? A reliable scholar of mystical theology, Père Augustine Léonard, sheds some light on the subject:

> This is due first of all to the fact that the mystic in the general structure of his life never completely abandons distinct representations. Besides it seems that in the wake of this experience of presence in obscurity, a content which transcends ordinary consciousness as well as its habitual means of perception, comes to substitute itself in the emptiness of negation. The indetermination is instantaneously overcome by a positive and personal content: Christ, God, the Trinity. Here psychology is reduced to silence, or else it can only accept the testimony of the mystics.
>
> For the living experience of negation and of the indetermination of distinct representations should logically end in unconsciousness, as so often happens to Hindu mystics. But with Christian mystics it never does so. It is rather that a new consciousness is born, which is in no way the individual or collective unconscious, but a superconsciousness. A dwelling place, already built but until now shut up, is opened in the mansion of the soul.[3]

Christian mystical experience is not the fruit of a direct and systematic effort, but is a gratuitous gift of God. The end sought is the perfection of love and not, as in other mysticisms, a mysterious path to transcendental knowledge. Let me recapitulate by quoting Père Leonard once more:

> The subjective and objective indetermination of mystical experience is explained, under pain of being an unconsciousness, only by a positive content. This content is referred to the dogmas of the Trinity and the Incarnation which give to Christian mysticism its personal character. From the reference to dogmas arises the question of the essential or accidental bond between dogmatic faith and mystical experience. A series of implications between experience and ideas indicates, even at the level of phenomenology, that this bond is not accidental, nor the fruit of a presumption. If one abstracts the mystical experience from the dogmatic statements in which it is cast, one disfigures it, empties it of its historical significance and deprives it even of its psychological specificity.[4]

Charles Davis seems right, then, to suggest the use of religious experience that is broad enough to embrace code and cult. *Religious feeling* would then refer to that element in religious experience that is a spontaneous, connatural response to religious reality, the vibration of our total being when we relate to the transcendent in and through religious activities and passivities.

> Religious feeling is the arousal of our personal being—our intelligent and bodily, spiritual and material selves—in what is, though variously mediated, a direct relation to transcendent reality. Religious feeling is constitutive of every truly personal religious experience, because without it religious responses are reduced to words, gestures, attitudes borrowed from others and repeated without personal involvement. By religious feeling a particular experience is intrinsi-

cally, not just extrinsically, for example merely ver-
bally or socially, religious.[5]

Since the transcendent is not an object within the world of
human meaning, religious feeling has an intentionality which
plunges us into darkness and involves us in a response to mystery. Religious images and concepts refer only indirectly to the
transcendent. Their function is to mediate the felt presence of a
reality that remains unknown and to foster the appropriate affective response.

What can this hidden object be, this truth beyond of consciousness, which can hold the attention of the soul to something unknown, beneath the trite and the commonplace, which can in-
flame the will to a degree surpassing all eloquent considerations
of the reason? It can only be the idea of God, presented to
consciousness in a new mode, or rather without mode. According to Blessed John Ruysbroeck, a Flemish mystic of the four-
teenth century,

> Many abide in error, so that they come not to con-
> templation, or to that which has no mode. Yet every
> hindrance is within themselves. They are disquieted
> at heart, watching narrowly the deeds of others, con-
> cerning themselves with the cares of their friends and
> kinsman in which they have no part, careful for their
> own necessities, wherefore the riches of God are veiled
> from them.[6]

It is in apophatic contemplation where the ideal of God has
been formed negatively, that we find the true mystical type if we
can exclude what may be termed philosophical contemplation or
speculation. The negative idea of God is the result of a process
of abstraction pushed to the ultimate. The aim of philosophical
speculation is knowledge, the aim of mystical contemplation is
love

The philosopher labors upward, climbing from negation to negation until he attains the ultimate of denial. Although his result expresses the Most Awful Actuality, the only Ultimately Real, He Who Is, in consciousness it remains the emptiest of notions, only dimly recognized, if at all, in the denial of all given experience. For the mystic this negative idea is the finger of the Most High touching his inmost being, and his heart blazes at the touch. He does not seek to know. "I am the most foolish of men and the wisdom of men is not with me. I have not learned wisdom, and have not known the science of saints" (Prov. 30:2-3). For the philosopher the kenosis of consciousness is but a dialectical process, for the mystic it is a vital necessity that his heart may feel what his mind cannot grasp.

There is something new and different going on in the mystical experience. The negative idea of God acts directly on the will without prior formulation as a word of the understanding. It is the will which vitally reacts to the negative idea of God by an act of love and in that act, the intelligence gleans knowledge.

As the fourteenth-century author of *The Cloud of Unknowing* insists, God may be loved but not, properly speaking, thought. He is reached by an affectivity that draws us beyond the whole world of human meaning, beyond all the objects of human thought. All our images and concepts of God must be relativized, even those representing God as personal.

The prereligious sense of our own fragility, our limits, our finitude, the awareness of the nothingness that surrounds our human existence becomes religious when the nothingness is experienced as positive, as indeed more real than the objects of the world of human meaning.

America's Spiritual Crisis

The mystic must not be confused with the psychic. Psychics are people who are in touch with another world, the world of

Psi, which includes three major categories: extrasensory perception, psychokinesis, or mind over matter; and survival
phenomena. Psychics are not necessarily spiritual; they may
have unusual faculties of perception and be familiar with the
beings and ways of a more glorious world than our own, but this
is a matter of faculty and knowledge, not of spirituality. If you
want to enter into the fantastic world of Psi you have simply to
enlarge your experience. If you want to become spiritual, that is,
wise, happy and free, you will have to learn from your experience.

The mystic is the one person most surely in touch with this
world of flesh and blood, of hard facts and concrete realities.
The spiritual world, if we must use the terms, is *this* world, and a
spiritual experience is what we are experiencing at this moment
if we look at it the right way.

It is obvious that we are presently witnessing a psychical revolution, one, in many respects, that has won the approval of science (biofeedback, body consciousness, metapsychiatry, neuro-
science, paraphysics, etc.), and one that could, if properly guided,
improve our human condition, and expand our human consciousness immeasurably. There is little evidence, however, that
a spiritual-mystical renewal is going on, despite Vatican II and
the subsequent changes in the Church.

It would be appropriate, I think, to speak as Spengler did
more than half a century ago, of *the Decline of the West*, except
that it appears now to be an irreversible stampede to destruction.
What is at stake is not the means to survive, not even the will to
survive, but the faith to survive. Was not our Western civilization
born of the great drama enacted in Palestine two thousand years
ago, the drama of the Incarnation, the Passion and the Resurrection and all the ramifications of that latter world-changing event?
It was this divine drama that inspired the great art, music, literature and architecture that have and will be the glory of our
civilization. Our martyrs, mystics and saints were inflamed by

the one single fire of Pentecost. We stake our lives and our loves on the "victory which overcomes the world" (I John 5:4)—the victory won by the Risen Christ.

Some remarkable lay voices such as Malcolm Muggeridge's and Alexander Solzhenitsyn's have recently cried out in dire warning: If Western man should now reject these origins of his civilization, persuading himself that he can be master of his own destiny, that he can shape his own life and chart his own future, then assuredly he and his way of life and all that he has stood for and stands for must infallibly perish. Muggeridge says:

> In other words, the real crisis which confronts us is about faith rather than power, about the question "Why" rather than the question "How"—about man's relationship with his Creator rather than about his energy supplies, his currency, his balance of trade and Gross National Product, his sexual fantasies, and his other passing preoccupations with which the media interminably concern themselves. These are essentially trivial matters easily adjusted when the need to do so is apparent, as in time of war; whereas the God we serve, the salvation we hope for, the light we live by in this world, and, when we come to leave it, the vista reaching before us into eternity—these concern the very fundamentals of our moral existence.[7]

It may be more constructive to speak of the modern human predicament in terms of a crisis rather than a decline. The Chinese word for crisis is made up of two characters, one meaning danger, the other opportunity. A crisis environment ought to be energizing, ought to be a time of idealism and sacrifice and great effort.

The contemporary American situation may be described as a mystical or spiritual crisis. A crisis in contemplation. The frenzied tempo of Sammy running, the waist-high culture of our schizoid society, the disintegration of education, the loss of our roots in nature and in home life, the loss of symbols, of community life, of integrated personalities, of uproariously happy people, the degradation of sex and matter (air and water pollution and the rape of the land)—these characteristics of the American way of life are far from being unrelated. On the contrary, they are manifestations of one central fact: an impoverishment of man's mystical life.

Man is naturally contemplative. But his mystical powers, left unexercised for so long, are seriously atrophied. They can and must be reactivated if man is to become himself, an integrated personality, and if his world is to become humanized and God-centered. The mystical way is the only proven way known to man for changing human behavior radically and permanently. And yet, the one central treasure of the Church that less than one tenth of its members knows anything about, is its profound and incomparable tradition of mysticism and contemplation.

According to Aldous Huxley's *Grey Eminence:* "The mystics are channels through which a little knowledge of reality filters down into our human universe of ignorance and illusion. A totally unmystical world would be a world totally blind and insane. From the beginnings of the eighteenth century onward, the sources of all mystical knowledge have been steadily diminishing in number, all over the planet. We are dangerously far advanced into the darkness."[8] A civilization that denies the place of mysticism or shuts out the possibility of it sets us inevitably on the road toward a philosophy that is not so much a "love of wisdom" as a hatred of wisdom. Everywhere there is activity. Everywhere there is busy-ness. Everywhere there are organization, projects, and programs.

But they emerge from an inner self that is not quite at home or at ease with itself, but rather acts and thinks and judges from its superficial spheres, from the achievements of mere intellect or mere calculation, or from the impulses of power, possession or pleasure. Activity without contemplation is blind. Action of any kind—political, economic, social, religious—is not wise except for proficients in the art of prayer. Louis Lallemant, S.J., a reliable spiritual guide of the seventeenth century, says: "If we have gone far in prayer, we shall give much to action; if we are but middlingly advanced in the inward life, we shall give ourselves only moderately to outward life; if we have only a very little inwardness, we shall give nothing at all to what is external. A man of prayer will accomplish more in one year than another in all his life."

A generation before Lallemant, the greatest and most reliable of all spiritual guides, the sixteenth-century Carmelite reformer St. John of the Cross said that those who rush headlong into good works without first having acquired through contemplation the power to act will accomplish little more than nothing, and sometimes nothing at all, and sometimes even harm.

The depths of man have to be revived again; man's soul has to be rediscovered. Everyone must have, as a permanent and constituent part of his life, prolonged periods as well as moments of his day when he becomes still and contemplates, among other things, himself, and with the living heart and soul asks himself one of the innumerable questions he has suppressed during the busy day. An atmosphere of prayer, the literature of the world's great religious traditions, manual labor, and tranquil creative activities should serve as a moving center in which to recompose the personality that has been disintegrated into a thousand threads and to reweave that personality into a proper unity.

The person has to pull out of the human anthill, the asphalt jungle, the daily chase; he has to become present to himself. He cannot give what he does not have. Self-possession is not the end but it must happen en route or one will never get to the end, at least not a distinctively worthy human end. Only a deeply contemplative attitude can permit a person to take a strong stand against the powers of time and of the world around him.

The central religious thrust today is dominated by a transcendental hunger and thirst for God—a hunger not very often or very well fed by the Church. Countless Christians have left the Church because they were not being nourished on the contemplative bread of the Mystical Body of Christ, on the Spirit, but were being regulated by the rules and roles of religion.

The theologians, bright with flaming talents, taking the world seriously, developing their science in a contemporary style, creating fashionable theological trends, have become celebrities. It is a heady experience. Theologians have become wordmongers instead of Word-listeners, that is, mystics. They are shockers, straining to tell the people something new, novel, contrary. What we need are shock absorbers—receiving, assimilating and digesting the eternal, single Word of God.

People are fed and sustained by a mystical theology; they are amused and confused by any other. Yet they are being led thoughtlessly from one vogue to another. It's so tempting to be faddish, accommodating; to leave our solitary, silent stance before the source of wisdom and become washed out in the "sauce" of endless meetings, parties, dialogues, lectures, conventions.

It's so easy to blame the old myths, the old symbols, the old structures. But where does the trouble really lie? In our own routine barren experience of the Truth. "See Christ and you are a Christian; all else is talk," said J.D. Salinger. "Be still and see that I am God" (Ps. 46:11). "Where there is no vision, the people perish" (Prov. 29:18). We will never see God as long as we refuse to stop, take time, enter into positive leisure or holy repose, and contemplate him.

We will miss him in the busy hustle-bustle of our groovy liturgies. We will miss him in our hurried, routinized, self-centered, vocal prayers. We will miss him in our frenzied apostolates. We will miss him, above all, in our education, whose goal is supposed to be contemplation, according to Plato, Socrates, Aristotle, the Fathers of the Church, Thomas Aquinas, and any ancient or modern educator worthy of our attention. Our word "school" comes from the Greek word "scholē," which means "leisure." The Greek schools provided the opportunity and established the discipline necessary for contemplation. Today our schools have expelled leisure, and American students, in years of education, never learn to cultivate the attitudes and predispositions needed for contemplation. Mysticism demands generosity, self-denial and stamina. This is the stuff of saints, I know. But if inspired and led—and that's the business of the Church—people will rise to this level in a crisis. In the meantime, religious and political leaders must do everything they can, as quickly as they can, to create a social environment favorable to contemplation. We must require of our ecclesiastical and civil leaders that they be mystics themselves, that is, men and women of prayer, of intuition, who know God by experience. Only the vision of God can make us wise. Without mystical vision, our education is a farce, our civilization a sham, religion an opium, liturgy a corpse, theology a fad, and the apostolate the most popular and pietistic escape from the God who said, "Be still and see that I am God" (Ps. 45).

Notes

[1]Charles Davis, *Body as Spirit: The Nature of Religious Feeling* (New York: Seabury Press, 1976), p. 13.

[2]St. John of the Cross, Prologue to the "Ascent of Mount Carmel," in *The Complete Works of Saint John of the Cross* translated by E. Allison Peers, Vol. I (London: Burns Oates & Washbourne, 1947), p. 11; See also, Prologue to the "Living Flame of Love," *Complete Works*, Vol. III, pp. 15-17.

[3]Augustine Léonard, "Studies on the Phenomena of Mystical Experience," in *Mystery and Mysticism: A Symposium* (London: Blackfriars Publications, 1956), p. 95.

[4]*Ibid.*

[5]Davis, op. cit., p. 25.

Chapter 2
Our Rational Prison

What is it that kills contemplation and makes the passionate life of Christian mysticism so difficult to enjoy? The causes are multiple and complex. But there does seem to be a matrix, which I would designate as rationalism.

There are, no doubt, marginal trends away from the dominance of rationalism. Astrologers, occultists, seers, evangelical witch doctors, and therapists can invent what they wish in order to find believers. When people stop believing in God, said British author G.K. Chesterton, they do not believe in nothing. They believe in *anything*. Despite the "new narcissism's" growing popularity, however, rationalism's supreme position of influence remains uncontested.

The Rational Bulldozer

With both precision and panache, Chesterton diagnoses the ravages of rationalism. "The madman," he says, "is not the man who has lost his reason. The madman is the man who has lost everything except his reason."[1] Chesterton goes on to extol the sanity of the poet who accepts everything as a gift from God and basks leisurely in the mystery of the ineffable Being, while the rest of us try insanely to bulldoze our way rationally into the secret of being, ruthlessly tearing the world to shreds in our frantic foolish effort to label everything in neat tidy categories that fit into our prefabricated logical framework. "The poet," says Chesterton, "only desires exaltation and expansion, a world to stretch himself in. The poet only asks to get his head into the heavens. It is the logician who seeks to get the heavens into his head. And it is his head that splits."[2]

Ultimately, as Chesterton knew so well, it is mysticism that keeps man sane—not the counterfeit that is catching the fancy of the masses today, but the worldly-minded, Christ-centered Incarnationalism that dominates the deepest and most authentic tradition of the Catholic Church.

As long as you have mystery you have health. Destroy the mystery and you create morbidity. The secret of mysticism is this: that man can understand everything by the help of what he does not understand.

> The morbid logician seeks to make everything lucid and succeeds in making everything mysterious. The mystic allows one thing to be mysterious, and everything else becomes lucid. The determinist makes the theory of causation quite clear, and then finds that he cannot say "if you please" to the housemaid. The Christian permits free will to remain a sacred mystery; but because of this his relations with the housemaid become of a sparkling and crystal clearness. He puts the seed of dogma in a central darkness; but it branches forth in all directions with abounding natural health. As we have taken the circle as the symbol of reason and madness, we may very well take the cross as the symbol at once of mystery and of health. Buddhism is centripetal but Christianity is centrifugal: it breaks out. For the circle is perfect and infinite in its nature; but it is fixed forever in its size; it can never be larger or smaller. But the cross, though it has at its heart a collision and a contradiction, can extend its four arms forever without altering its

shape. Because it has a paradox in its center it can grow without changing. The circle returns upon itself and is bound. The cross opens its arms to the four winds; it is a signpost for free travellers. . . . The one created thing which we cannot look at is the one thing in the light of which we look at everything. Like the sun at noonday, mysticism explains everything else by the blaze of its own victorious invisibility. Detached intellectualism is (in the exact sense of a popular phrase) all moonshine; for it is light without heat, and it is secondary light, reflected from a dead world. . . . But that transcendentalism by which all men live has primarily much the position of the sun in the sky. We are conscious of it as of a kind of splendid confusion; it is something both shining and shapeless, at once a blaze and a blur. But the circle of the moon is as clear and unmistakable, as recurrent and inevitable, as the circle of Euclid on a blackboard. For the moon is utterly reasonable. And the moon is the mother of lunatics and has given to them all her name.[3]

Rationalism thwarts the enjoyment of the fullness of humanity. We are inordinately impressed by the scientific method. To observe certain phenomena and then to put two and two together is a legitimate form of knowledge; but it is merely one of the ways in which the mind can function. Though we have managed to master a large segment of reality by such intellectual manipulation, we have, at the same time, become slaves to a certain limited concept of mind. Unlimited reserves of physical force have been harnessed; but because the suprarational powers of the mind have been left untapped, we remain unwise and are afraid of our own self-destruction.

Using the mind as a calculating machine not only makes nuclear disaster an inevitable threat to the world community, it impoverishes every one of us here and now. When reduced to

merely rational power for the sake of intellectual domination
and possession, the mind deadens what it touches.

The substitution of mental concepts for living experience
keeps the exigencies of life at a safe distance. That is what the
Scribes and Pharisees did and Jesus lashed out at them, de-
nouncing them as vipers and hypocrites. They had reduced
Moses and the prophets to a conceptual system safely possessed,
and behind this shield they protected themselves from the impact of the Living God. It would take a mighty prophet not to be
stifled and stunted by the system.

What was always a temptation has become in our technological
society almost a necessity. Man has been turned into a
mind-machine and is expected to function as such in a collectivity
organized for that purpose, in a society of objects ruled by objects. Even sex is now governed by the principle of noninvolve-
ment or objectivity.

So much of the rebellion today is directed against organization
as such, against the very principle of rationality and the rigidity
it imposes. If man is forced into rational molds, and his life
fenced about with formulae, he will, as Dostoyevsky says in his
Notes from the Underground, "go mad on purpose so as to have no
judgment and behave as he likes."

Without sufficient self-feeling we are bound to become addicts
of one sort or another. When so-called progress in America
broke up the tribal bonds of the Navajo Indians, isolating them
from their felt environment, the Navajos began eating peyote in
a desperate effort to recapture a sense of identity.

What American economy did to the Indians, rationalism has
done to us all. It requires us to be so detached from the object of
our perception that both we and the perceived objects are reduced to lifeless abstractions. Such a cerebral approach to reality
precludes the contact and involvement we need to live deeply
and fully.

Separated from our feelings, we are bound to suffer an intol-

erable personal impoverishment that will drive us into the raven-
ing hands of a manipulating pedagogue, an emasculating dem-
agogue, or a ruthless technocracy. Robbed of our own personal
identity, we mask ourselves behind the identity of the cause we
have espoused. We will defend this cause with our lives and take
the lives of those who seem to threaten the very thing that provides us such a respectable substitute for living. We get all
wrapped up in the cause and tend to forget the aching isolation
at the core of our being.

The Old Testament story of Job is to the point. As long as Job
remained under the sway of his rationalist friends and felt compelled to match his experience of life with his preconceived
theories of what he was and what he deserved, he was miserable
and confounded at every turn. But he managed to cling tenaci-
ously to his own experience of reality. This creative fidelity to
life and opposition to an existence based upon projections of his
own fantasies rewarded him with a final and fulfilling peace.
The Lord spoke to Job out of the whirlwind. Reality was revealed to him first hand in all its terrifying power and ruthless-
ness. It smashed to smithereens the smug rationale he and his
friends had carefully concocted in their heads.

In the throes of thoughtfully lived out experience, Job died
and was raised from the dead. There was no more whimpering
about the injustice of life. The terror and delight of it all simply
left him awestruck and full of wonder: "I have dealt with great
things that I do not understand; things too wonderful for me,
which I cannot know. I had heard of you by word of mouth, but
now my eye has seen you. Therefore I disown what I have said
and repent in dust and ashes" (Job 42:3-6). Job risked the security and certainty of a carefully worked out theory of existence
and suffered his way into a rich and rewarding experience of
life.

There is a world of difference between knowledge as possession and knowledge as communion. You can collect enough data

about a person, place or thing to give you a certain secure possession of their abstract truth. But that's not the same as being in love with the person, at home in the town, or in union with the thing. What you lack—and this is the worst kind of impoverishment—is living communion with the elusive mystery of the person, place or thing.

Our contemporary preoccupation with knowledge as possession has led us into a sterile cul-de-sac. We are dying from lack of communion. The Word was made flesh so that we might have vital contact with an embodied God. It is not enough to know about God, we must know him in the flesh, in the intimate and experiential contact that comes with communion, and in no other way. Such deep profound communion with the mystery of Being, the Eternal Word, gives life. "I am come that [you] may have life, and have it more abundantly" (John 10:10). We will not give up our false security in what the mind dominates and possesses for the sake of the living knowledge which is communion, unless we are willing to follow Christ into total poverty, into death, so that God can raise us up above isolated unassimilated fragments of truth into contemplative union with Truth itself.

This loving awareness through divine union demands no permanent withdrawal from the hurly-burly of the world. This resurrected state of mind does not hold the world cheap. On the contrary, absolutely everything is prized and cherished with a new intensity and immediacy hitherto unknown. The place where we feel most at home, the people we most deeply love, the works of genius which have most fired our imagination, these are the instances of the Word being made flesh and dwelling among us, and thus creating us; leading all the time through "the cloud of unknowing" into more and more mysterious realms of reality. We are wooed into the secret mystery of Being by love. Communion, the very heartbeat of life and love, is precluded whenever we take someone or something by force and turn it into our intellectual property. An unfortunate displacement has occurred in religion itself, a shift from knowledge as communion to knowledge as possession. According to the latter we believe in a creed and are saved by carefully possessed orthodoxies and dutifully practiced techniques. According to the true Christian way, however, we are made whole by waiting expectantly for ever new opportunities to be with God. We do not believe in a creed. We believe through a creed in a person. That person summons us into an enlightened and transcendent openness. There is no way, thank God, to package the mystery into a collection of verbalized concepts.

In Christ we behold passion at its highest pitch; communion between God and man. Rationalism is our foolish attempt to cage that experience. The meaning of the Christ-event is beyond the cognizance of the intellect-bound mind. It can be apprehended only intuitively and imaginatively as the life of the Jesus-watchers, the Word-listeners comes to consciousness. All attempts to decode Christ's parables and demythologize the Gospel myths lead inevitably to a strawman Jesus and a dead Christianity, which is perilously close to what we've got. No one can live for very long on abstractions or fall in love with dogmatic propositions or formulas of the faith. We live or die for communion with God, not for a theology of God. "This is eternal life, that you may know God and Jesus Christ whom [he] has sent" (John 17:3).

The problem of evil, perhaps more than anything else, helps us out of our rational imprisonment precisely by being a strict logical self-contradiction in religious understanding. Yet, as the story of Job or the life of Dostoyevsky illustrates, such a conclusion need not induce us to reject the traditional Judeo-Christian belief in God or in his providence. Many of us are reasonable enough to see the absurdity of conventional belief in God, moral

enough to be deeply disturbed by it, but religious enough to
believe in and act on promises logically false, practically self-
defeating and contrary to common sense.

As Ralph Waldo Emerson once remarked, a foolish consis-
tency is the hobgoblin of little minds. "God offers to every mind
its choice between truth and repose," he said:

> Take which you please—you can never have both.
> Between these, as a pendulum, man oscillates. He in
> whom the love of repose predominates will accept the
> first creed, the first philosophy, the first political
> party he meets—most likely his father's. He gets rest,
> commodity and reputation; but he shuts the door of
> truth. He in whom the love of truth predominates will
> keep himself aloof from all moorings, and afloat. He
> will abstain from dogmatism and recognize all the
> opposite negations between which, as walls, his being
> is swung. He submits to the inconvenience of sus-
> pense and imperfect opinion, but he is a candidate for
> truth, as the other is not, and respects the highest law
> of his being.[4]

The madman latches on to one particular truth so rationally
and so rigidly that all other truths and the connections among
them evade him, and so he is driven by the clarity of that single
isolated truth into the loony bin.

> *No* concept, not even those of mathematics, is abso-
> lutely precise; and some of the most important for
> everyday use are extremely vague. Nevertheless our
> instinctive beliefs involving such concepts are far
> more trustworthy than the best established results of
> science, if these be precisely understood. . . . Men who
> are given to defining too much inevitably run them-
> selves into confusion in dealing with the vague con-
> cepts of common sense.[5]

The touch of God is the richest experience open to man. The cumulative traditions of mankind, through their myths and symbols, have tried to preserve the meaning of such crucial moments of intercourse between God and man. Man is naturally anxious to clarify what is unclear in his comprehension of the religious myths he inherits, and it is inevitable that in doing so he will experience paradoxes like the theological problem of evil that appears when he tries to think clearly and consistently about the original mythopoeic revelation.

Experience as deep as the religious one cannot be expressed adequately except through ambiguous and self-contradictory signs. The content of the experience far exceeds the boundaries of reason. We are lucky to have the problem of evil! It interrupts our conceptualistic and relatively abstract approach to God, and introduces us to the existential response to pain, suffering and absurdity. The ubiquity of evil reminds us of our own mental and moral limitations.

Theologians should certainly be up-to-date and able to communicate effectively with the contemporary world. But if they become overly anxious to be accepted in the scientific and philosophical communities, they may sacrifice the sort of passion-in-the-face-of-paradox that is one essential characteristic of Biblical religion. In that case, they give up the characteristic intensity of religious passion, the fire of the prophets and the saints without gaining any real philosophical or scientific advantage.

The answer to the problem of evil is not a set of propositions or straightforward assertions but an unexpected change in the quality of our individual existence. Our own ethical-religious crises lead us beyond speculation into concrete absurd reality. Once we get out of the suburbs of reality and immerse ourselves in life, in radical confrontation with the brute, earthy surd of existence we stop fretting rationally about whether or not God exists; instead the paradoxical name of God is wrung from us.

Then we will know the monumental difference between trying to fit God into our heads and being headed off by God—into suprarational realms of being that the speculative mind knows nothing about. We will no longer chatter with casual academic aplomb about God, but will speak awesomely from experience, like Job, with a scorched tongue.

Machiavellian Madness

The quintessence of rationalism is Machiavellianism, a moral disease as old as fallen mankind.

An article in the popular *Psychology Today* pointed to the global spread of Machiavellianism today.[6] The magazine printed a series of assertions that had been devised to test our degree of Machiavellianism. Among them were: "Anyone who completely trusts anyone else is asking for trouble." "It is safest to assume that all people have a vicious streak and it will come out when they are given a chance." "Most men forget more easily the death of their father than the loss of their property." The National Opinion Research Center, which used this short form of the test in a random sample of American adults, found that the national average was 25. The lowest score—for the non-Machiavellian—was 10. According to author Richard Christie, industrialization and urbanization apparently contribute to an emerging generation of Machiavellis—worldwide.

A version of the test was given to fifteen groups of Spanish students from nine provinces. Scores were closely related to the degree of provincial industrialization. The test was also translated into Mandarin Chinese and given to high-school students in Hong Kong. Those attending a Westernized school, where the language of instruction was English and where the curriculum followed the British system, scored higher in Machiavellianism than students attending a traditional (Confucian) Chinese high school.

A Machiavellian score, of course, represents only the degree to which a person believes that people in general are manipulatable. The high scorer does not necessarily claim that he would, or does, manipulate. However, researchers inferred that agreement with such cynical views of human nature might go along with the emotional detachment and amoral attitude necessary for successful deception.

Just as sadism, another form of human behavior as old as sinful man received its name and its theory from the Marquis de Sade, so did Machiavellianism take on a proper name and become a political technique with the publication of *The Prince* by Niccolò Machiavelli, an Italian statesman and political philosopher who lived during the sixteenth century.

The Prince is a manual for tyrants. It was Joseph Stalin's bedside companion and is still read as a text in practical politics. Nixon, his administrative assistants, his unofficial White House chaplain, and his Jesuit speech-writer must have read it. The principles governing President Ford's settlement of the Mayagüez affair could have been lifted verbatim right out of *The Prince*.

When we read *The Prince* today we are shocked by the shameless and unscrupulous way Machiavelli proposes to settle things by a violent use of power. But the far more disgusting fact is that his pragmatic and cynical doctrine of the importance and conduct of war is exactly the same as accepted in practice today in the international power struggle. Virtue, Machiavelli warns, has ruined many a prince. Better to rely on force and be feared rather than be loved.

Admittedly, there is something refreshing about the Renaissance author's style: the power tactics are expressed with such primitive and clear frankness, free from all the euphemism and neologisms that have reduced so much recent political discussion to double-talk. Our Renaissance man claims quite unabashedly that cruelty is better in the long run. It works. It produces. He uses Cesare Borgia as an example. This is cool violence, respectable immorality, and not at all, as we have so recently and shamefully witnessed, incompatible with American utilitarianism. The argument of our present-day political pragmatists is exactly the same when they assert that the only hope of peace and order is "to tough it out," regardless of moral offenses, with the hardest and most intransigent policy.

As Thomas Merton points out in *Seeds of Destruction,* power is an end in itself. Persons and policies are reduced to means. The chief means is war, not a "just" war but a victorious war. The important thing is to win. Spectacularly muddled thinking; and, obviously, a murderous and immoral approach. But is it any different from the clammy and camouflaged statements of our own political administrators who have learned to express themselves with less brutal bluntness? As Clausewitz manages to say, even though he is a political spokesman of modern times: "To introduce into the philosophy of war a principle of moderation would be absurd. War is an act of violence pursued to the uttermost." We abhor Hitler publicly and admire him secretly. But the secret is out, at least for anyone who has ears to hear and eyes to see behind the jargon of the military-industrial power structure, the public image of the politicians, and the platitudes of the churches.

Just as sadism is the contamination of eros by perverted sexual behavior, so Machiavellianism is a deformation of politics by a dehumanizing technique. We are presently enthralled by that technique. There are no religious prophets or political saints who seem willing or passionate enough to break out of and strongly oppose this collective enthrallment.

Once politics divorced itself from Christian morality and wedded abstract reason, the birth of technique was assured. With technique came the repudiation of reasonable expedients in favor of a single rational principle, and an abandonment of changing and discontinuous relationships in favor of rigid and abstract law. Technique thrusts us back into a regressive form of legalism and formalism made absurd and obsolete once and for all by the liberating Passion of Christ who created a whole new world of brand-new men who can remain human and become progressively human only by moving into further reaches of freedom.

Machiavellianism is not only spreading geographically and getting a stronger hold on the political world; it has become much more than a political affair—what to do so as to win and consolidate power. It is now a pervasive factor influencing and shaping all relationships between men, political and nonpolitical. All human activities have been transformed into techniques; politics have become supreme. The Church itself is not immune as it succumbs to the Machiavellian temptation to subordinate all moral and religious considerations to the conservation and defense of the ecclesiastical institution. This marvelous human experiment called the Church, inspired by Christ and organized by his early followers, has obviously failed insofar as it has not produced a Christian world. It produces hybrid Christians, but they aid and abet the Machiavellian regime. What is the use of training the best runners in the world if the track is so constructed that they've got to run the wrong way?

The immediate and practical result of Machiavellianism is immense but unjustifiable. Hitler and Mussolini died ignominiously after causing incredible catastrophe in Germany and Italy. The great democracies of the West joined the victory, but emerged from the ordeal in a worsened condition. Stalin's Russia was invaded and devastated by the armies of his German ex-ally. The only result of the universal and indiscriminate practice of Machiavellianism in modern times has been to provoke the two biggest wars in history, as well as the most foolish one, and to bring infinite suffering and enormous destruction to mankind. Despite all this, and our present human predicament in America, there are no signs of a Machiavellian decline. This staggering dilemma should induce some vigorous reflection, which in turn should evoke prayer—an awestruck cry of the heart—that would issue, I am sure, in radical and dynamic forms of religious renewal that have thus far hardly even been hinted at.

It seems impossible to become un-Machiavellian, that is, to subordinate politics to a higher principle. Eros has been aborted, Agape repressed. There is something wrong with human activity on a deeper and more subtle level than man's politics. Man as man has been denatured; and this debacle engulfed us with the culminating, demoniac stroke of rationalism, forcing politics into wedlock with abstract reason, political science with technique. Through the linking of politics and technique and our uncritical subscription to that prostitution of the human polity we all pitch in and by our own pseudoreligious efforts heighten the capacity of the technological institutions to complete the dehumanizing of mankind.

Institutions today are so monstrous that even strong, inspired leadership (nowhere in the offing) buckles under the pressures of the techno-barbaric juggernaut. Even the leaders we now have who seem so mercenary and mendacious do not, I am sure, conspire against us. They are simply victims of the institutions they serve, institutions that move in only one direction, and their principal energies digest, assimilate, rationalize and dehumanize any and all reform. Should I pray or vote to get good men into high positions of the State and Church when these very positions, in the words of Hosea, make all men "detestable like the things they loved" (9:10)? How do we tolerate institutions so blatantly uncongenial to the people? It seems that just enough incidental good accrues to the people as a by-product of the machinery of the State that weary folks are palliated. Whatever education anyone manages to get is also incidental.

I am tempted to say the same about spiritual growth in the Church; but I can't. In the Church, thank God, there is a supernatural impediment: "I am with you always" (Matt. 28:20). "The gates of hell shall not prevail against it [the Church]" (Matt. 16:18). But whatever growth there is usually happens despite our paltry programs, our evangelical crusades, and our charismatic movements. So many of the things we do for the institutions we identify with, are exercises in idolatry and futility. Machiavellianism nurtures the seeds of violence. Reason is overemphasized. Other human faculties are de-emphasized. All of them are made to function as ancillary to reason. Reason, of course, is an important faculty, a condition without which no truly human activity happens: but it is not, and cannot be, the substance out of which human destiny and wholeness are achieved. Reason latches onto some object outside of man, obsessively and slavishly pursues that object as an end, and turns man himself into a means for attainment of that end. If man proves to be inadequate, he is dismissed as a useless means. If reason escapes from its auxiliary sphere, it tyrannizes and dehumanizes man, while it makes the end the well-being of the nation, the factory, the school, the parish, the family.

Apart from God—though even he is not a separate being from man—there is no end outside of man; to posit one is absurd. But reason balks at man as an end because the mystery of man cannot be ransacked, manipulated, categorized, exploited with immunity. Reason has a field day with the State precisely because there is nothing ineffable about it. The way man is used in the modern world is ruthless, cruel and ludicrous; but it is rational. Contempt for man is the fundamental characteristic of the modern world, in spite of the superficial courtesy games and welfare programs that abound. Our contemporary art, literature, film and poetry are stressing this depressing feature of our society: it is absurd—a hellish maze with no exit.

Is there any difference between an educated boy going off to war and a bull in the arena if man is not an end? What difference does it make who becomes President if the nation or the company goes on functioning under the rigid auspices of rationalism? Under our present regimen the pimp who sells the prostitute's body for profit is as justified in doing so as the head of State who declares war on another State. In both cases reason reigns supreme, achieving its brothel or war-victory using man as the means, in one case as prostitute, in the other soldier.

The most rational and surely the most effective way of getting rid of a headache is to cut off the aching head. The rational approach is to attain the end—getting rid of the headache—most effectively. The effective way is violent: chopping off the head. To achieve the end man uses himself. But if the end is man—to be himself again by alleviation of the headache, he takes an aspirin; less violent, less immediately effective, but human. The final happy end is a result of being irrational, or better, suprarational, that is, loving oneself more than reason.

If reason is the end, we are left with two choices: persuasion or violence. But persuasion must confront too many nonrational elements: respect for the individual, loyalty to tradition, openness to religion and mystery, aesthetic feeling, charity, compassion and sympathy. Why not choose violence which is, after all, in perfect harmony with abstract reason? Logically, the most rational means for attaining an end other than man is man himself, that is, the use of violence as a means implies man as means—and implies contempt for man.

Suppose I am asked by the Canadian government to build an airstrip in the center of the U.S. on a tract of land purchased from the U.S. by Canada. I study a map and pick the best brains—geographers, architects, engineers, aeronautical experts. We select, according to the dictates of reason, the best possible place with the least expenditure of time, energy and money. There are two ways open to me. I can make the airstrip my end and follow the calculations of reason all the way, even if it means using man as a means and uprooting a whole village in the process. Or I can choose as my end the people whom the airstrip is meant to serve. If that is my choice then I will have to redesign my project so that their parks will not be spoiled, nor their rivers polluted; and I must see to it that all the salutary aspects of village life enjoyed and treasured by the people are left undisturbed. In this case, what has happened is that love of people has prevailed over the purely rational end of building an airstrip. Humanness has triumphed over reason.

According to Machiavelli, the end justifies the means; and man is the means. So from now on he will owe his survival on earth uniquely to his use as means. But the use of man as a means will lead either to the extermination of families and races or to the total extinction of man. We will all end up as soap or lampshades. The earth is littered with the ruins of civilizations that perished because they degraded man from the status of end to that of means.

But, as Italian author Alberto Moravia says, even if you burn man, he will always leave a residue. Use him, degrade him, crush him—no matter how you debase him you will always find a residue, in which there resides, however unactivated, a sacred character. Suffering is the residue. And it is the one infallible sign of sacredness. That is why the Bible finds more dignity and nobility in man as a "suffering servant" than as a "rational animal" or a "thinking reed." Even Pascal, who had one foot in the illuminist camp, was compelled to say: "The heart has its reasons which reason knows nothing of."

By suffering I do not mean any and every kind of pain but a suffering born of a sense of profanation, sacrilege and degradation which man, who regards himself as an end, feels when he is reduced to a mere means. Such suffering is the lot of man today amid the ugliness, brutality and banality of city life. Man's finest achievements are used for his own further degradation (e.g., technology).

In other words, if you experience suffering when used as a means, you know you are a man. It is this noble sense of oneself as an end that transforms suffering and empowers it to be liberating, purifying and cathartic. Man should not suffer from being a means; he should suffer from not being an end. To suffer from being a bureaucrat or a worker or a soldier is a passive moral position; to suffer from not being a man is an active moral position. That is what Léon Bloy meant when he said that the only unhappiness is not to be a saint. Man needs to establish as his end an image of himself—and that's what Christ is for—against which he can measure his strength and suffer from falling short of.

This is a healthy existential anguish, not a crippling neurotic anxiety. This is how suffering leads to and is transformed into joy. And that is why joy dominates the Gospels and any authentic Christian way of life. The source of joy is man's unfaltering recognition that he is an end, along with sufficient opportunities to act in character—to be himself. You find this supremely in Jesus: a perceptively keen consciousness of who he was—his Father's Word, object of his love—and, therefore the refusal to be had: "No one takes [my life] from me, but I lay it down of my own accord" (John 10:18).

Without this loving awareness of himself as an end and the freedom to act the way he thinks, that is to say, leisurely and creatively, man necessarily falls into despair. And what is modern man's most telling sign of despair? Activism.

In the history of mankind every depressed age is charac-terized by activism—shallow, feverish, uninspired activities that do not enrich or enliven the spirit of man. That is why you also find a peculiar phenomenon occurring in those flaccid periods of history: a return to the desert, to solitude and simplicity, to an ascetical-mystical life. The reason for the flight to the desert is a very positive one and has saved the character and the repressed nobility of mankind in every decadent epoch. It is simply this: the resurrection and redirection of vitality inhumanly dissipated in the use of man as a means.

The vast majority of mankind will, of course, not choose to flee but will remain mesmerized by the sophisticated stupefaction of the Machiavellianized herd. What happens to them is predictable. The historical pattern has repeated itself with remarkable consistentcy. This depraved condition, no matter how common and acceptable, triggers in their incorruptible, noncombustible, indestructible depths, a human alarm. Acting out of mass impulse instead of solitary wisdom there is a stampede. The very actions that led the herd into despair in the first place are multiplied hysterically and the despair, naturally, is increased. So our present human predicament can be summed up thus: the predominance of action over contemplation. The predominance of action over contemplation constitutes the secret drain on the modern world. The proliferation of "prayer houses" in the Church is not the solution. Concentration in the area of prayer and worship, however, does indicate, encouragingly enough, a recognition of the central problem. Somehow or other we have got to transfer human energy from one place to another, not just among religious groups but within all the thick, messy layers of our whole fleshy world, our flabby society.

Notes

[1] G.K. Chesterton, *Orthodoxy* (New York: Dodd, Mead, 1944), p. 32.
[2] *Ibid.*, p. 29.
[3] *Ibid.*, pp.49-51.
[4] As quoted in *Knowledge and Value*, edited by Elmer Sprague and Paul W. Taylor (New York: Harcourt, Brace & World, 1967), frontispiece.
[5] Charles S. Peirce, "The Concept of God" in *Philosophical Writings of Peirce*, selected and edited by Justus Buchler (New York: Dover, 1955), p. 376.
[6] Richard Christie, "The Machiavellis among Us," *Psychology Today, IV* (Nov., 1970), 82ff.

Part II: Liberation

Chapter 3
Soul Friending

The difficulties encountered in the mystical life are so great, each man's ignorance of himself so vast, that some kind of guidance becomes imperative. "The most dangerous man in the world is the contemplative who is guided by nobody," said Thomas Merton, the Trappist monk from Gethsemane, Kentucky.

Theologians and psychologists of the spiritual life have always agreed on the necessity of spiritual direction. At the very origin of the Church we find a well-known manifestation of this. Although Saul, breathing out threat and carnage, heard the voice of Christ himself and asked: "Lord, what would you have me to do?" he was sent for the answer to Damascus, to Ananias. "Go into the city; and there it will be told you what you must do" (Acts 9:6, 7). St. Teresa of Avila advised everyone "to consult some learned person if he can, and the more learned the person the better. Those who walk in the way of prayer have the greater need of learning; and the more spiritual they are, the greater is their need. . . . I, myself, through not knowing what to do, have suffered much and lost a great deal of time. I am sorry for souls who reach this state [the prayer of quiet] and find themselves alone."

The Value of Personal Direction

Personal direction does not produce the mystical experience but prepares us for it. We need spiritual direction even to begin the spiritual life. Without it, there is often no beginning at all. We begin unsteadily, unsurely, and out of false principles. The interior life is like getting an airplane off the ground, that most important moment in the whole flight. The plane is readied: help for a successful take-off comes from every direction. Once off the ground and in the air all is well. Everyone relaxes.

Something similar happens to the human being on his spiritual journey. Once lifted into the supernatural order, led by the Spirit, all is well. But help is needed in the beginning. Just as the pilot has a general knowledge of aeronautics but needs particular, concrete knowledge applied to his situation here and now, so the Christian in pursuit of perfection needs, at the beginning of his spiritual life, a specific, concrete application of principles, here and now, to a given situation, a particular kind of nature, temperament, disposition.

Perfection, it is important to remember, has different forms, according to the vast variety of personalities and the particular circumstances and conditions surrounding each one. When this is overlooked by the unwise and undirected, undesirable consequences follow. Someone imitates a saint slavishly and stifles the growth of his own unique personality. Another forces himself into a mold and experiences frustration, spoiling his humanity. Another applies the rules of spiritual growth without discrimination and so foils his best efforts and thwarts his finest qualities. The results, in general, are disastrous. To avert them, one does not always need a director, but one does need direction.

Spiritual direction is particularly helpful during the precarious periods: transitional stages of prayer, scruples, temptations, doubts, darkness, and crises of all kinds. It is an aid to perseverance, since most of us are often tempted to give up. We need periodic checkups for stimulation, correction, and encouragement, to provide orientation and balance to our lives, to preclude unwholesome periods of excessive elation or depression. Direction frequently saves us from merely going through the motions of religion. Many Christians do not appreciate the dignity of their mystical vocation. Many have almost no idea of the immense love of God for them, the personal nature of that love, and the power of that love to bring them profound human fulfillment. The seeds of this mystical life are planted in every Christian. But seeds must grow and develop before the harvest is reaped. There are thousands of Christians walking about the face of the earth bearing in their bodies the infinite God of whom they know practically nothing. Many people in the Church stand on the threshold, go through the external motions of religion, and dutifully profess their faith. But never have they entered into the heart of the Church where the Living God dwells. They do not enjoy their faith; they do not know God by experience.

The Christian religion must come alive in each individual life. A person needs more than abstract knowledge. He needs to know God firsthand. He needs to go through the arduous process of loss and gain, trial and error. But the mystical life is dangerous. We ought not to risk it alone. Since few of us can live with risk, we stand on the threshold, fulfilling our "obligations" but missing the joy, the power and the glory of religion. That is why G.K. Chesterton said: "Christianity has not been tried and found wanting; it has been found difficult and left untried." If we would only come all the way in and drink of the eternal fountain of life bubbling up at the heart of the Church!

Spiritual direction helps the person become himself—his best self. Self-deception is common and easy. We are fooled and ruled by our own defense mechanisms for escaping the truth about ourselves. We are afraid of the harrowing experience of self-knowledge. We walk the tightrope of ambivalence, patting ourselves on the back, but admitting vaguely to being less than we ought. Laziness is transformed deceitfully into an "easygoing temperament." Anger and impatience become "righteous indignation." The multiplication of prayers becomes a "spiritual life." Self-constructed ideals of holiness allow our passions to run riot.

John of the Cross attributes a lack of spiritual growth to the absence of spiritual direction because we do not understand ourselves and lack competent, alert directors to guide us to the summit. This is not God's fault, St. John is quick to add: "When God says or reveals something to a soul, he gives this same soul to whom he says it, a kind of inclination to tell it to the person to whom it is fitting it should be told. Until this has been done, there is not entire satisfaction because the man has not been reassured by another man like himself." A layman or woman who takes seriously the command to be perfect needs spiritual direction even more than the religious, since he does not have the benefit of monastic life, and as a rule is subjected to more worldly pressures. St. Paul went to the apostles to be confirmed in his faith. The Fathers of the Desert, in spite of an insatiable thirst for solitude, gathered together for the sake of direction. Most saints had spiritual directors; all of them had some kind of direction.

If spiritual direction were no more than a curb to self-will, it would be invaluable. As Merton writes in *New Seeds of Contemplation*, our own will often becomes the source of so much misery and darkness that we do not consult another man merely for light, wisdom or counsel: we come to have a passion for obedience itself and for the renunciation of our own will. "A spirit that is drawn to God in contemplation will soon learn the value of obedience: the hardships and anguish he has to suffer every day from the burden of his own clumsiness, incompetence and pride will give him a hunger to be led and advised and directed by somebody else."

But spiritual direction goes far beyond the curbing of self-will. No one can know himself by himself. "Who constitutes himself his own master becomes the disciple of a fool," said St. Bernard. No book can substitute for the wisdom of a good director. If spiritual direction is to be effective, the one directed must live in a spirit of faith, seeing God in his director and responding to God through him. No good will come if the subject treats spiritual direction as a luxury or the director uses it merely as a means of "laying down the law." Those directed may seek sympathy on occasion but never a confirmation of their self-pity. To reduce spiritual direction to the pleasures of pleasant conversation is nothing but a waste of the director's time. Spiritual direction is not meant to be an evasion of responsibility nor an imprimatur on arbitrary behavior and moodiness. Its purpose is rather to learn how to decide, sometimes what to decide, but never not to decide.

Childlike candor and honesty ought to characterize the personality of the one directed. He must open himself with confidence, particularly in the case of supernatural favors. St. Teresa and St. John of the Cross are very emphatic: all must be revealed—totally, but simply and briefly, and only for the purpose of being directed, not of being praised, admired or pampered.

Apart from cases where people take a vow of obedience to their director, it is evident that there can be no question of obedience in the sense of strict precept or canonical obligation. But there is a traditional opinion that a person benefits by complete submission for a certain period of time. During certain trials and crises, particularly when scruples are involved, this submission is necessary as part of the spiritual remedy.

Should a director be retained throughout life? If possible, it is usually desirable, but never with the same permanence, regularity and dependence as in earlier stages of the interior life. No matter how advanced a person may be, no matter how enlightened, strengthened and comforted by the Holy Spirit, he may yet depart from the Way, the Truth, and the Life. He may become attached in some subtle way. He may mistake the consolations of God for the God of consolations. He may slacken his efforts, rest on his laurels, look for rewards here and now. Hence he may sometimes profitably turn to others for guidance, hoping all along for a guide of sufficient maturity and sympathy.

Is it wise to change a director? If the director has become a hindrance rather than a help, we ought to change. But such change should never be prompted by a fitful or temperamental inclination. Change for the sake of change ought to be opposed by both the old director and the one newly approached.

The clumsy title "spiritual director" seems almost entirely unsatisfactory. The Celtic penitential book came up with a far more appropriate one: "soul-friend" *(anmchara)*, and hastened to add that "Anyone without a soul friend is like a body without a head."

In the early ages of the Church, especially among the Desert Fathers, a soul-friend was called either *pneumatikos pater* or *abba*, and was expected to help shape the lives of his children. As a "spiritual father" he exercised genuine "paternity" by engendering in his "child" the life of the Spirit which alone enables us to become true children of God. For "all who are led by the Spirit of God are the sons of God" (Rom. 8:14).

A comparable word in the Russian tradition is *staretz*, in English "starets," which means "old man" and implies the number of years needed to become a soul-friend. "A staretz," says Dostoyevsky in *The Brothers Karamazov*," is one who takes your soul and your will into his soul and will." There can be nothing casual or careless about the relationship between two "friends" involved in "soul-care."

Nothing less than a very personal heart-breaking betrayal occurs when, after years of "soul friending" at a crucial juncture, a risky moment, a precarious situation, a glimpse of Calvary, an unpleasant discovery about oneself, the frightened or wounded soul walks away from the anguished *staretz* (and the

Way of the Cross), never to return again. Only a brokenhearted mother or lover can know what that is like. The awful thing is that it can, and often does, happen to a *staretz* or a soul friend countless times. It may be the deepest possible affliction for a person who takes his pastoral care seriously. He must face this fact squarely ahead of time and be prepared for some disconcerting experiences.

Each time he takes a person into his direction, he accepts from God a spiritual responsibility which may cost him heavily and bring physical and psychic exhaustion, darkness, tremendous vicarious suffering, and the cross. In offering himself as a director, he offers to take his part in the saving work of Christ, the mysterious redemption of the world through suffering and death. Each person entrusted to his care brings a need which he must meet, an opportunity so unique it will never be repeated, a duty that perhaps no one else can fulfill.

The saints were remarkably and refreshingly effective spiritual directors because they were utterly uncalculating in their self-giving and cared for souls with unbounded love and an eagerness to suffer. They show us that spiritual direction involves something more than pat answers, pious clichés, and ready-made remedies. It is, rather, a rugged piece of work, and demands a costly self-surrender to God for the work he wants done in others. Supporting those entrusted to him and entering into their secret joys, fears, sorrows and temptations, the spiritual director accompanies Christ to Gethsemani and Calvary and shares with him the crushing weight of the human condition and the burden of sin.

Between soul friends, as the term suggests, there is always a certain kinship, a certain emotional rapport. There is, in fact, often intense love and faithful devotion on both sides. Yet the spiritual director is always the director, and his penitent never loses sight of the fact.

A penitent can become the friend of his director only if he is already sufficiently integrated as a person himself with a relatively elevated degree of emotional maturity. Otherwise all efforts at profound communication with the strong personality of his director (the director must be strong to be a soul-friend) will risk the loss of the penitent's selfhood. Instead of a self-actualized person in search of direction, he may become a mere imitator or sycophant and have nothing to offer in dialogue with his director.

Ignace Lepp, a priest and praticing psychotherapist in Paris until his death in 1966, spoke of soul-friending in terms of the master-disciple relationship. According to him,

> To meet a master who wishes to become our friend is a great opportunity in life. Thanks to him we shall be able to actualize our principal powers to the maximum. The man who has confidence in himself, far from refusing to be a disciple, freely chooses the master he believes most suited to help him become himself. If there is an art of being a master, there is also an art, scarcely less difficult, of being a disciple. The most effective masters generally began by being excellent disciples.[1]

The soul-friend is freely chosen, and his relationship is a continuous one. The relationship is not one of equality, but the director and his student should be faithful friends. There should be on the part of the student, an affectionate confidence in the director, a loving response to his personal qualities, upon which his direction depends.

St. Teresa found particular consolation and joy in her directors. She was solicitous and attentive to them and lavished upon them deep and faithful regard, expressed with warmth and simplicity. This attitude was no threat to her purity of heart; it was the result of her self-mastery. Not only in the case of Teresa and John of the Cross but also between St. Francis of Assisi and

St. Clare, St. Francis de Sales and St. Jane Frances de Chantal, Blessed Jordan of Saxony and Blessed Diana d'Andalo, for example, the relationship between director and directed led to a warmhearted, holy friendship. Father Lepp points out that in his own experience "friendship between an older master and a young female disciple seems to be . . . the most exquisite form of friendship between men and women," since "young, educated women, more often than their male colleagues . . . are generally intellectually less proud and thus recognize more readily their need to be guided."[2]

Finding a Soul-Friend

If we choose our doctors, lawyers and teachers with care, how much more carefully we should choose our soul-friend. The orientation of our lives, the rapidity of spiritual ascent, our contemplation and mysticism can depend upon the choice of a spiritual guide. St. Francis de Sales recommends that a soul-friend be chosen, not among a thousand, but from ten thousand. The choice should be governed by reason and faith, not merely our natural inclination.

St. John of the Cross says: "It is a difficult thing to explain how the spirit of the disciple grows in conformity with that of his spiritual father, in a hidden and secret way." St. Teresa stressed, "It is of great importance that the director should be a prudent man—of sound understanding, I mean—and also an experienced one; if he is a learned man as well, that is a very great advantage." Elsewhere she says: "If such a person be in the world, praise God that he is able to choose the director to whom he is to be subject, and let him not give up such righteous freedom; let him rather remain without a director until he finds the right one." God himself sometimes indicates the right director to one he has charged with a special mission. St. Paul was sent to Ananias; St. Margaret Mary to Blessed Claude de la Colombière.

We should look for soul-friends in nearby monasteries or among the priests of our own parish. The parish priest cannot administer the sacraments in a detached, routine sort of way and presume that his pastoral work is done. He must offer personal insight and earnest love to suit his people's individual needs until Christ's image is finally formed in them. The parish priest must not excuse himself from the responsibility of spiritual direction by claiming "Not necessary," "Better to be just an ordinary Christian," "Too advanced for me," or "No time," "Too busy."

The soul-friend need not be a rare and unique kind of priest. It is the great privilege and high calling of every priest to be a director of souls. In fact, if I were asked what, above all, is the priest, I would be inclined to answer: a soul-friend. But spiritual direction is bound up especially with the personal qualities of the priest. We would sin through imprudence by counting solely on his sacerdotal grace and not considering his aptitude for the special ministry of giving regular direction. Oftentimes brothers, sisters, and lay people make better directors. Baron Von Hügel, a married man with three daughters is a famous example. Anglican mystical scholar Evelyn Underhill is another.

We should look for five qualities in our soul-friend: personal prayer and holiness, reverence for the mystery of every human person, prudence, experience and learning.

1. *The soul-friend must be holy:* Christ-conscious and a God-centered man of prayer.

It is only by faithful personal attention to God, constant and adoring recourse to him, confident humble communion with him, that a director's work can be effective. The upkeep of this life-giving contact with the eternal world, this secret intercourse with the living Christ, is a primary duty he owes to those he directs. The loving, enraptured vision of God, the limitless self-forgetful confidence in God, the generous desire to give unstintingly for his purposes—these are the sources of the devoted energies of the true director.

His first duty is to see to it that he himself is an authentic, integrated person. He must be real and take hold of existence by keeping in deep touch with ultimate reality, by a profound communion with the Spirit in whom "we live and move and have our being," (Acts 17:28). From this communion he will draw spiritual food and fresh air and supernatural sunshine, which God gives not so much for the sake of its consoling warmth and light, as for the thoughtful but invisible chemical rays which give spiritual vitality. The soul-friend cannot achieve this by his own anxious efforts. But it will be given him from on high if he looks steadily in the right direction, prays, and accepts the inward discipline with the necessary preparation.

2. *The soul-friend must revere the mystery of every human person.*

He must regard every human being as sacred and stand with immense, awful fear, and reverence before the mystery of the person and the even more wonderful mystery of God in a human life. St. John of the Cross has severe words for spiritual guides who "like rough blacksmiths know only the use of the hammer," and bids them remember that "Here the Holy Spirit is the principal agent and the real guide of souls, who never ceases to take care of them and never neglects any means by which they may profit and draw near to God quickly and in the surest way." This is a delicate business, and no task for hardheaded, coldhearted people. The whole purpose of any human instrumentality is to lead the person to that degree of sanctity where he or she is totally docile to the ultimate Director, who alone is holy, the Holy Spirit.

God rarely leads any two people by the same route to him. The soul-friend must be keenly aware of how unique each path and each person is. St. John of the Cross exclaims: "Hardly could we find one that even half resembles another."

I once lived near a mansion where only one of the many gardeners employed had succeeded with every one of the roses. I asked him the secret of his success. He told me that the other gardeners treated all the roses not unwisely, but too generally. They treated them all in precisely the same way; whereas he himself watched each rosebush separately, and followed out for each plant its special need for soil, manure, sun, air, water, support and shelter.

The soul-friend needs to treat each person as distinctly and carefully as that. Immeasurable damage has been done by directors (and this includes superiors) who have advised or governed with a sameness, a coldness, a generality that kills creativity and originality; who have imposed upon their charges lifeless systems and humorless programs that are outworn, incompatible, unsound, and most undesirable; and who have, therefore, robbed from the people they directed or governed the very foundation for any kind of greatness or nobility—*the spontaneous zest for life.*

The poignant lament that man is being despoiled of his personality is for all those busy with endless classifications of good and bad, for those who think they know everything about their brothers and sisters in religion, their subjects, their fellow workers, their employees, who don't respect sufficiently God's mysteries in dealing with souls. This is the most subtle form of that desolating scandal that so horrified our Lord. Better to be bound and cast into the sea than be the source of this kind of direction. It is a great privilege for the holy soul-friend to comtemplate the work of God in others, and to collaborate discreetly, always in the shadow, so that the power, mercy, and wisdom of God, admirable in all his works but especially in his saints, may shine forth and be glorified.

The soul-friend is nothing but an instrument in the hands of God. St. John of the Cross teaches: "The spiritual guide of these souls must consider that the principal agent, the real guide in such an office, is not himself, but the Holy Spirit who never ceases to watch over them. He is nothing but an instrument to direct them in the way of perfection according to the lights of faith, and according to the gifts that God has accorded to each of them." His role is not the same as that of the teacher of the human sciences. The professor is appointed to teach philosophy, literature or mathematics, which reveal only the conclusions of reason.

The soul-friend does have recourse to certain precedents: he learns how to pray, to discern what is sinful, to mortify himself. This is horizontal direction. It is useful, and it bears fruit, but it is not sufficient in itself. There must also be vertical direction which considers the grace proper to the one being directed. Although the continual advancements of psychology permit us to delve more deeply into the mystery of the individual, there still remains a zone which will escape scientific explanation. The soul-friend will never penetrate that zone except with the light which God alone can dispense. As St. John of the Cross says: "The spiritual director must content himself with preparing the soul to receive God. He must restrain himself from going too far and from seeking to build the spiritual edifice. This role belongs entirely to the Father of Light."

"Only God can deify," said St. Thomas Aquinas. A director is but a servant. His attitude must be that of John the Baptist: "He must increase, but I must decrease" (John 3:30).

3. *The soul-friend must be prudent.*

He must never confuse the positive, dynamic, manly virtue of prudence with spineless caution. Prudence is the art of taking risks. It does not always choose the safest means to the end, but the best and most appropriate here and now.

The soul-friend must be bold, daring and decisive, and at the same time exquisitely delicate. He is confronted continually by the darkness of the divine and the complexity of human nature. He must cope with the demands of God and human weakness. He will need to expend all of his spiritual might and wit toward discerning God's will. The discernment of spirits is so crucial that it is probably proper to say that it is the heart of true soul-friending.

Rashness and hastiness are always perilous. So are complacency in one's own judgment, perfunctory observations, unwillingness to admit a mistake or to change one's mind, to reverse a decision. Though he must not be crippled by hesitation or undue delay, the director must be prepared to *wait*. The great doers are often the most patient, watchful men. He must attune the person to God's pace, God's goal, God's manner. He must be awake, alert, responsive. He must not only think and pray. He must study, sweat, labor, worry, weep, bleed, and, above all, love.

Prudence aims at adopting the actual possibilities of the person to the demands of God and not using up prematurely the forces that are necessary for a long journey. This makes for sustained effort and saves a reserve for unpredictable obstacles, when all the energies of the person can be mobilized for the sudden crisis. The prudent soul-friend must not command impossible things but neither must he, in the words of St. Teresa, teach us how "to be toads" and to be "satisfied if our souls show themselves fit only to catch lizards." Discretion is not timidity or laziness. It knows the exigencies of Divine Love and aims to respond to these graciously, wisely, without compromise, and only rarely with violence.

The prudent director will be the soul's friend through the maze of life's complications, marking the present duty, determining attitudes, and pointing out the plan of Providence. He must avoid, however, any kind of monopoly, expoiting persons for his own private ends, petty jealousies, and a narrow authoritarianism that makes him impose his own views or methods and diminishes the liberty of the human person under the action of the Holy Spirit.

Prudent soul-friends must hold what they have received in

confidence in strict secrecy. St. Teresa says, "They should be advised to keep their experiences very secret, and it is well that their advisers should observe secrecy too. I speak of this knowledge, for I have been caused great distress by the indiscretion of certain persons with whom I have discussed my experiences in prayer. By talking about them to each other they have done me great harm, divulging things which should have been kept very secret." On the other hand, however, the prudent soul-friend may and ought at times, seek authorized counsel.

4. *The soul-friend should be a man of experience.*

It is impossible to overestimate the value of experience in a director. All the masters of the spiritual life have spoken from their own experience or from that of persons they have been able to observe closely. Techniques and methods cannot track down the action of God in a person; they may even hinder his action and restrict it. Without experience a soul-friend can be a kind and passive witness, but it does not seem that he can—without enlightenment from God himself—encourage and direct with authority as his function obliges him. Even the signs of contemplation of St. John of the Cross need to be experienced in some degree before judicious application can be made to concrete cases.

We know how indebted St. Teresa of Avila was to experienced directors: St. Francis Borgia, St. Peter of Alcántara. She says: "I have come across souls so constrained and afflicted because of the inexperience of their director that I have been really sorry for them."

An inexperienced director may easily thwart once and for all the soaring spirit of the soul, either through lack of understanding or timidity; or again by letting it exhaust itself prematurely by excessive mortifications. There is no substitute for experience. Most tragic mistakes in direction are made by young, ardent, but inexperienced directors.

5. *The soul-friend should be a learned man.*

A thorough grasp of the basic principles of ascetic and mystical theology is indispensable to anyone who wishes to give enlightened help. The soul-friend must not be so captivated by or absorbed in one branch of theology or one aspect of the spiritual life that he loses his balanced perspective of the whole: for instance, a liturgist who knows nothing of contemplation, or a contemplative who ignores the liturgy. He must possess a unifying synthesis of all theological science. There are no partitions among dogmatic, moral, ascetic, and mystical theology. There is a science of God and his dealings with men, branching out in different ways but always demanding a fixed center.

St. Teresa had a real penchant for learned men as directors. She preferred them even to pious men. "The more learned the better," she said. And not just ordinary learning: she had no use for those pseudointellectuals who couldn't explain the manner of God's presence in the soul and spoke of "timid, half-learned men whose shortcomings have cost me very dear."

It is not enough to know theology. A soul-friend must also know psychology, that science which opens up the mysterious realm of the subconscious. St. John of the Cross is the great psychologist of the spiritual life. He should be read and reread. Modern psychology has made an enormous contribution toward the understanding of the whole man, but in this field especially, a little knowledge is a dangerous thing.

Soul-Care

The soul-friend is more than a teacher; he is an educator in the full sense. He presents the principles of the spiritual life, not in the abstract or in general, as in the classroom, in lectures, or in sermons, but in the concrete: applying them here and now to the individual. He urges the individual on by arousing fervor and strengthening the will, ensuring that the directed will not stop at resolution but go on to action, and eventually be able to guide himself more readily.

The soul-friend should help to map out a general rule of life. He should suggest the best and most appropriate and timely spiritual reading (see the section entitled "Not by Bread Alone" pp. 136-142). He should offer specific and practical recommendations for overcoming temptation and practicing virtue. Since he is dealing with human beings who are rooted in organic life and deeply colored by their surroundings, expressing themselves as embodied creatures, he cannot afford to disregard, even for an instant, the life of the body (see section on "Biblical Sensuousness," pp. 120-126).

Since spiritual direction has traditionally been both prophetic and critical, it can help us withstand the constant pressures of human respect, public opinion, and the pull toward mass conformity, opportunism, the world, the flesh and the devil. It aims at conformity with the will of God and not conformity with social institutions or a majority of human beings. Against the mediocre world it bears testimony and is a living witness. Like monasticism itself, spiritual direction adopts a critical posture toward this world and its structures. Spiritual direction has always been closely identified with monasticism and shares the monastic prophetic sense. It therefore cannot possibly serve the mendacious mentality of the organization man; nor can it be a soft and solipsistic pastime for pious ladies or whimpering half-men who crave pseudospiritual conversations with unwed priests.

Some of the best features of soul-friending were lost during the Counter-Reformation period and after the Council of Trent. The soul-friend tended to become one who settled cases of conscience. The influence of canon law and juridicism led to major distortions of the tradition. But there were also some positive contributions, thanks to St. Ignatius of Loyola and some of the "Exercises" he introduced

Soul-friending has almost always been closely linked with the

sacrament of penance. This association has been freely em-
phasized by the revision of the Rite of Reconciliation in the *Ordo
Penitentiae* of 1974, which stresses warmth and kindness, friendship and trust, healing power and growth in the Spirit—
language which has replaced the juridical language of Trent.

Although soul-friending should not be equated with counseling, the process of reconciliation often necessarily involves a
degree of counseling. Counseling emphasizes the development
of understanding rather than the imparting of information. The
understanding sought is self-understanding or insight. The
counselor's function is to educe the art of thinking — in this case,
self-analysis — rather than to impose his own way of thinking
upon his friend. He is not there to solve problems but to produce changes in the friend that will enable him to make wise
future decisions as well as to extricate himself from his immediate difficulties. The counselor aims at changing attitudes as
well as actions. Counseling inevitably involves personal relationships. It is difficult for a person undergoing counseling to
understand why the thinking he does in the counseling situation
changes his life more than the thinking he does about his problem by himself at home. Actually, it is the relationship with the
counselor—his soul-friend—that makes the difference.

The art of spiritual advice and every form of human counsel
consists for the most part in an ability to establish rapport and
achieve union; in other words, to love objectively in an intensely
searching and probing dialogue. The relationship between two
soul-friends is unquestionably one of deep significance, but it is
most of all a matter of the giving or withholding of the selves of
both. The degree to which both commit themselves to this relationship seems to determine the success of the whole process.

There must, therefore, be a true giving of self—first of the self
of the soul-friend and then a genuine commitment of the person
coming for help, more slowly but just as surely, as he gains
confidence. This is what constitutes a relationship of both loving

and being loved, an "I-Thou" relationship. Obviously this is not love in the popular emotional sense. Rather it is a type of *amor benevolentiae* —a love that gives of itself entirely and seeks no return from the other except his best fulfillment of himself. Inextricably bound up with this mutual commitment is not just the director's isolated intellect, but his whole power of love-knowledge. To understand at the deepest level of another's feelings and responses is an immeasurably more profound, complex, and delicate kind of understanding than simply knowing the meaning of the words he uses. This is what a person really means when he says after an interview, "You know, he really understood me"; and this is the quality of genuine praise and respect which is conveyed when someone is called "a very understanding person."

The soul-friend who is a counselor has a great vantage point. Everyone knows that when you are uninvolved you can usually see things more clearly than the one who is involved. You see, so to speak, from a different angle or point of view. Or, to put it another way, the person presents his "inner view," usually interwoven in a complex recitation of the experiences, reactions, and feelings he had at the time.

The soul-friend can be very helpful if he gives back in his statement or response the "interview," that is, the awarenesses that he gets by analyzing in his uninvolved, reasonable way, the basic feelings, attitudes, goals, and fundamental motives and values that are at the core of each series of reactions as he communicates them.

So the first act of the soul-friend is to give of himself. Permeating and suffusing his whole counseling process are a recognition of the extent of human weakness and also a respectful and optimistic confidence in a person's ability to change or better himself, that is, to operate at a higher level of reason and self-control. It is important to remember, however, that no matter how many psychological techniques we use, we cannot come to know and understand another person merely by way of rational knowledge.

There is only one path into man's inner secret, and that is the way of love. Love actively penetrates the other person, quelling the desire to know by union. I know the other, and I know myself, I know everybody, and I know nothing. I know in the only way in which knowledge is possible for me—by the experience of union, not by any knowledge my thoughts can provide. The only way to full knowledge lies in the act of love; this act transcends thought, it transcends words. Just as the only positive knowledge we can have of God comes by way of an intuition born of love (contemplation), so the only positive experimental knowledge we can have of another human being is of an intuition born of love (contemplation). No amount of psychological insight can take the place of love. It can lead to it, prepare for it, make it possible—and this is the legitimate function of psychoanalytic work—but it must not try to be a substitute for the responsible act of commitment, an act without which no real change occurs in a human being. The spiritual director must become one with his penitent, and at the same time retain his own separateness and objectivity so that he can formulate his experiences in an act of oneness and separateness at the same time.

Such a relationship extends beyond both soul-friends to the divine dimension. It is not two but a Third who shares intimately in this pastoral counseling relationship. The soul-friend must never forget nor overlook his secondary and subordinate role, never regard his own personal activity and talents as a basis for apostolic success. Consequently, counseling, understanding and skill, in addition to their positive qualities, can be a most delicate means by which the soul-friend checks his own egotism and thus recognizes his own human limitation. In this secondary and subordinate role, then, the soul-friend using every possible psychological aid, spends himself for others in such a way that

God's place and his own reasonable insight may be productive of a more adequate psychological and spiritual integration in time and eternity.

There should be no confusion between spiritual direction and secular counseling. The context for spiritual direction is the Christian community; its nature is theological; and its essential *locus* is worship. Clinical models are not appropriate. Among other things, the director is a sort of physician. But this is an analogical concept and not a central one. Spiritual direction is not concerned with pathology; nor is it concerned essentially with emotional disturbances, but with the achievement of health, wholeness and sanctity for the whole community.

A good soul-friend helps us avoid the common mistakes and the typical pitfalls of the spiritual life. He preserves us from that pride which overestimates our own achievements and forgets that mysticism is an utterly gratuitous divine gift. He protects us from the delusion that our experiences are mystical when they are not. St. Teresa offers some sage advice in her *Interior Castle:*

> At times, indeed, very often this may be nothing but a fancy, especially with persons of a lively imagination or who are afflicted with melancholy to any marked extent. I think no attention should be paid to such people when they say they see, hear, or learn anything supernaturally.[3]

A good soul-friend steers us clear of hyper-introspection, self-consciousness, and quietism. He will not let us fanatically forget the end and multiply the means, fixating at one low level of spiritual growth. Neither will he allow us to live presumptuously, skipping the preliminary stages of growth because we become falsely preoccupied with the end without having become sufficiently and suitably disposed through the purgative process.

The prudent soul-friend reminds us of the love behind a constructive asceticism and recommends an intelligent, organic, ongoing, gradual and gracious program of mortification. He leads us away from "strong man" acts of asceticism which destroy rather than regulate our body-person. With St. Benedict, he helps us understand that in general all things are to be done in moderation.

As the life of grace develops, the soul-friend helps us to distinguish pure contemplative gold from counterfeit subjective phenomena. He will not let us confuse contemplation with the somatic marvels which sometimes accompany mystical experiences. These are often attractive to a temperament which seeks after "signs and wonders." In general, the soul-friend will not allow anyone to place any importance upon visions and revelations, but will urge him simply to recollect himself with simplicity in God when he experiences such phenomena.

The psychophysical phenomena—rapture, trance, ecstasy, cessation of the ordinary activity of the mind or the senses—that sometimes occur concomitantly at certain phases of the mystical life and during certain states of prayer, are by no means essential to the mystical experience. They are only accidental and secondary and must neither be sought after nor clung to, should they occur. They may well be due to an abnormal psychophysical temperament. They may be nothing but the natural effect of physical weakness, and the natural incapacity of the soul's lower functions to endure the special operation of God in the inmost center. When a man has purified or harmonized his lower functioning sufficiently, he may still enjoy mystical experience but without the usual psychophysical manifestations.

Any value that these experiences possess pertains entirely to an underlying spiritual communication from God through such phenomenal means. Since it is so easy to suffer delusion or even to cling inordinately to such consolations, the great mystics do not hesitate to urge everyone to reject them. If they are not treated with graceful, lighthearted detachment, they can, and often do, become impediments to mystical union. The good soul-friend will try to help eliminate these phenomena as soon as possible from the life of the person he is directing.

One of the most valuable aids a soul-friend offers is in the vastly important area of prayer (see Chapter 6, section on "A Cry of the Heart," pp. 146–154). People today are absolutely convinced of the necessity of daily prayer for the sustenance of any decent spiritual life. They are learning the art of prayer and are coming to recognize more and more the normalcy of mystical contemplation: knowing God by experience in a pure intuition born of love. A soul-friend must be sufficiently experienced and instructed in the ways of prayer in order to perceive people's needs which, after all, are quite simple, and provide the appropriate solution to their questions. He will need a clear and solid doctrine reduced to a few principles with practical, incisive directives to permit him to direct persons with prudence and security in the way of prayer, and even in the way of mystical contemplation, as well as to judge in what cases they should be encouraged to see a more specialized spiritual director.

If, for instance, a person complains that he cannot meditate, after a few judicious questions the soul-friend should be able to ascertain the causal factor: whether the incapacity to meditate be due to natural or supernatural causes, physical or spiritual, an unreal concept of meditation, sinfulness or carelessness, or finally the grace of God. The person who complains that he cannot meditate may simply mean that he can no longer think clearly about God. But St. Teresa teaches, in this regard, that prayer consists "not in thinking much, but in loving much," and ought to be simply a humble and spontaneous conversation of the soul with the Lord, a sort of colloquy in which one tells him freely all that he feels in his heart: his difficulties, anxieties, desires, and above all, his love for him. A worried person, upon hearing this, may begin to feel at ease once more and readily understand that he too is capable of meditating in such a manner. On the other hand, the inability to meditate at all can be very real, when a person feels great aridity which makes him incapable not only of producing good thoughts but even of stirring his heart; it seems to him that he is no longer serving or loving God. This may be due to no human cause.

The soul-friend can be an enormous help to the suffering soul at this point. He will recognize the sanctifying hand of God, who uses aridity to move the soul from meditation to mystical contemplation. Mystical contemplation here refers to a simple type of prayer in which the person, instead of reasoning and forming distinct affections, feels impelled to stop and recollect himself in a kind of simple loving attention to God that is very profitable for the interior life. Precisely because the Lord wishes him to be occupied in this way, he begins by making meditation impossible.

When aridity is prolonged in the faithful person of prayer, and at the same time he feels inclined to attend simply to God, the soul-friend advises him to leave off meditation and to accustom himself to remaining there contentedly before God, loving him, wishing only to offer him the most affectionate companionship, and bearing the trials which the spontaneous movement of the imagination brings about. His loving attention to the presence of God will in time become easy and meaningful. To be able to explain this to people is certainly to help them more efficaciously than simply to recommend patience. The soul-friend will nourish in such mystics the sense of total generosity: only in this atmosphere of boundless self-sacrifice can the mystic grace develop and reach full maturity.

John of the Cross calls this transition to contemplation "the dark night of the soul" and is relentlessly critical of directors who cannot competently guide people through the mysterious and painful experiences of nothingness it entails.

St. John is referring specifically to the life of prayer, but the same kind of transition, along with its darkness, occurs just as frequently and as precariously in other aspects of life. Competent directors are as desperately needed in these other areas. There is, for instance, a dark night of marriage that is seldom recognized as such, even by counselors. The failure to recognize the difficult transition to a deeper and more mysterious realm of love results in the disintegration of the marriage. Half the people I know who left the priesthood and religious life left because they were caught perilously in the dark night, which is really a sign of progress, but they didn't know it. The same thing happens in jobs, friendships and ministries.

The dark night involves tension and suffering and apparent withdrawal of the ordinary power of prayer. Skilled and sympathetic guidance is of special service to the soul, which is often confused and disheartened by its own experience, its strange sense of dimness and incapacity. Since this area is almost entirely neglected, it may be helpful to discuss in detail the experience of nothingness (*nada*) which is the essence of every variety of the dark night.

Notes

¹Ignace Lepp, *The Ways of Friendship* translated by Bernard Murchland (New York: Macmillan, 1966), p. 101.

²*Ibid*, p. 104.

³Teresa of Avila, *The Interior Castle or The Mansions*, translated from the Autograph of Saint Teresa, by the Benedictines of Stanbrook (London: Thomas Baker, 1906), Sixth Mansion, Chapter III, p. 155.

Chapter 4
The Experience of Nada

Nada is Spanish for "nothing." The experience of nothingness lies at the heart of the whole spiritual life. It is the beginning of the mystical journey.

Nada is the one mystery where all religious traditions of both East and West converge. John of the Cross and others sum up the spiritual life in terms of it. *Todo y Nada*. Unless you are detached from everything that is not God, you cannot belong to God. Unless you are emptied, you cannot be filled. Unless you lose your life, you cannot find it. This is why the first contemplative center of the Spiritual Life Institute in Sedona, Arizona, was named Nada. Our second foundation, a more primitive hermitage in the woods of North Kemptville, Nova Scotia, we call Nova Nada.

Nothingness may enliven or destroy those who face it, but those who ignore it are condemned to unreality. They cannot pretend to a real life which, if it is full of real risk, is also full of promise.

The Sense of Nothingness

We need not be afraid of nothing. We cannot have something without nothing. If there were no space there would be nothing solid. Without space outside there would be no solid edges. If there were no background of space there would be no photo, no discernible image. The solid and the space, the figure and the background are inseparable and go together.

There is no animosity between nothing and something. "To be or not to be" is *not* the question. Contrasts such as black and white, life and death, pleasure and pain, up and down are meaningful precisely because they belong together. Something and nothing are two sides of the same coin. If you file away the tails side completely enough, the heads side will also disappear. Nothing is the force whereby something can be manifested.

Form implies a void; a void implies form. Forms that appear to be solid are massive instances of energy. You cannot put your finger through the wall for the same reason that you cannot put it through the space between the blades of a revolving fan: it is moving too fast. The wall is nothing and form in motion.

There are no waves without troughs. In the case of day and night, life and death, the alternation of the waves is slower. The deepest me is the nothing side. The unconscious is the part of experience that is doing consciousness.

In an excellent article entitled "The Meaning of Nothingness" in *Desert Call* for Winter, 1976, Irish Carmelite Noel Dermot O'Donoghue maintains that experiences which involve a sense of nothingness are universal. They become more conscious and therefore more articulate in the transparent personalities of the child, the mystic, and the poet. They involve a sense of contingency: the realization that I might not be, that I might not have been, that there is no necessity for my existence. They include the constant threat, in fact, the inevitability of death, which makes life itself a mere possibility.

There is a big difference—and it's an important distinction—between being nothing and sensing my own nothingness. The first makes me less than mortal; the other places me among the immortals. I am something, but barely so; and therefore, because of my barely-so-ness, remarkably if not miraculously so!

But I am forever haunted by the inescapable *sense* of nothingness which is as positive and powerful as the sense of reality, as intimate and personal as the sense of self.

The dreadful, wonderful sense of our own nothingness grows out of contemplation, philosophical or religious, and issues in the fundamental human disposition of humility, ontological or Christian. In either case, we take a long loving look at our own reality and face our own nothingness. All good philosophers do this; and all decent philosophies are based on this radical recognition. At the same nothinged point, all the great religions are thrust into a Godward dimension.

Only being can affirm nothingness. It is that beingful part of me that witnesses and affirms all the ways in which I am nothing. And precisely because my fundamental transcendent self—the Christ in me—is able to acknowledge the nothingness of me, it lives in constant awe, wonder, and astonishment. In facing our nothingness, we affirm our greatness. Negativity is encompassed by a positive leap through and beyond it.

My sense of nothingness depends on my sense of being. I will never come to understand, in absolute and ultimate terms, how and why I am not, unless I see how and why I am. Only in the light of the really real can I discern and accept my own unreality. One is eternal and unchangeable; the other is subject to time and change. I am now, but soon I shall cease to be. My undoing has already begun and is well on its way. I am doomed to die—today, tomorrow, or a few years hence. My existence is so temporary and tentative! It is true to say I exist; but even truer to say I do not exist. I have been touched by existence, have possessed existence precariously for a brief span of time on this earth, and then lost it forever. How fragile my existence in relation to the immeasurable past and the incalculable future! It is the light of being that reveals my nothingness; if I do not possess this vision, then my sense of my own nothingness will never be entirely full and steady, and I shall never really possess my own being.

What a terrible deprivation—this loss of vision, of the light of being, and the consequent loss of self-possession. The shaky, spurious self comes up with a compensatory pathology. It tends to strut and preen, as its proud, haughty and self-conscious behavior accentuates the only fact it knows: "I am something." This, perhaps more than any other single factor, has ruined lives, families, and communities, and has spoiled vocations. If you are strutting and preening you cannot hear the voice of God; you cannot hear the truth revealed either by a spiritual director or a life situation.

It is highly significant that the handful of people I have known over the years whose spiritual growth and mystical lives I have found most impressive, are all extraordinarily tough-minded, rugged people in the rough-and-tumble dailyness of their lives, but extremely docile when it comes to spiritual direction. No wonder St. John of the Cross says that ninety percent of spiritual growth depends on docility. Most of the people I know who lost their vocation or their mystical way lost it because they were not humble.

What they lost first was their balance, a proper human perspective, a "meek and mild" attitude (however wild and vivacious), and then, inevitably, their vocation. A vocation can be regained if the fundamental human posture—humility—is recovered. As St. Teresa said, "Humility is walking in the truth." The rediscovery of humility will be based on an empirical common-sense observation: that I do not exist of myself, that I am not the ground of my own existence. Simply because of this I am, of myself and by myself, nothing; I am a mere limited possibility of existence.

As Noel O'Donoghue, O.C.D., points out, this metaphysical apprehension of my own nothingness goes deeper than my sense of contingency and facticity; it also goes deeper than death, for it is an apprehension of my present nothingness. Death is the apprehension of my future nothingness, though when death is seen as involved in my present condition, then the two apprehensions tend to coincide. This same vision of true reality as necessary and immutable reveals also the nothingness of the world around me. A spectacular sports event, a religious convention or a traffic jam is the frivolous froth of being. Nothingness lurks just beneath the swinging surface; and like my own nothingness, it is quiet, deep and eternal.

This kind of humility, the fruit of our apprehension of being and nothingness, is not come by easily. You don't glean it from books and professors. It is learned through experience, humiliation, dread, terror, suffering, and pathos. It is also learned through ecstasy and joy. No single event will open us up sufficiently to absolute, transcendent being. What is asked of us by the real is a lifelong exploration into the truth, discerning, as we move steadily onward and upward, the goodness of the truth. If the *goodness* of the truth escapes us, we will do violence to ourselves and others in the name of abstract truths.

The sense of nothingness is heightened and intensified and becomes most salubrious and fruitful when absolute reality or ultimate being is recognized as God. In comparison with him, in the light of his stunning reality, we are literally nothing. To be a creature is to be absolutely dependent, to hold one's being at every moment from another, to be of oneself nothing. This theme recurs constantly in the Scriptures; it is a basic element in man's religious consciousness.

A passage in the tenth chapter of the sixth book of St. Teresa of Avila's *Interior Castle or The Mansions* typifies the mystic's grasp of this crucial insight:

> Once, while I was wondering why our Lord so dearly loves the virtue of humility, the thought suddenly struck me, without previous reflection, that it is because he is the supreme Truth, and humility is the *truth,* for it is most true that we have nothing good of

ourselves but only misery and nothingness—whoever ignores this, lives a type of falsehood. They that realise this fact most deeply are the most pleasing to God, the supreme Truth, for they walk before him.[1]

It is obvious that St. Teresa, whose description of the greatness of the human soul is scarcely equaled in spiritual literature, nevertheless accepted wholeheartedly the theme of man's nothingness. Elsewhere she wonders how it is that God can have "so deep a love for so loathsome a worm" as man. The mode of expression differs according to time and place, but the experience is ineluctably the same: under the penetrating light of the divine being our defects show up mercilessly. If we are not comparably impressed with the divine love and mercy, we can be thrust relentlessly into depression and despair. As St. Teresa points out, in the Sixth Mansion the soul is lavishly blessed with illuminations of the divine truth in comparison with which all human truth seems like darkness. It was the experience of this illimitable Light and supreme Truth that enabled Teresa to understand why the Psalmist says, "Every man is a liar" (116:11).

This is no mere metaphor, for under the illuminating rays of Supreme Truth only absolute, uncreated being retains the status of being. All else is nothing, having in itself no power of existence. Only to the degree that I recognize and accept my nothingness am I something. On this nothingness of mine which is eternal and immutable, I can build a moral life that is impregnable and boundless.

There is something infinite about my nothingness. We all share it. We are surrounded by it. It permeates everything. The more vibrantly we live the more conscious we become of the inherent dissatisfaction of things, and we sing with John of the Cross in his *Spiritual Canticle*, "Send me no more/ A messenger/ Who cannot tell me what I seek" (Stanza 6).

Creatures are dissatisfying, not in what they withhold, but in what they give. Thérèse Martin, another Carmelite saint, speaks of this in her *Autobiography:* She recalls as a child her great joy was fishing with her father:

"He went out fishing sometimes, this Prince Charming of mine, and it was a great day when he took me with him; I did so love the countryside, with all its birds and the flowers. I even tried fishing, too, with a small rod of my own; but I preferred sitting there on the grass, with the flowers for my company. My thoughts went deep at such times, and although I knew nothing about meditating, my soul did sink into a state of genuine prayer. Noises came to me from a distance, the sighing of the wind, and faint echoes, even, of music from soldiers on the march, inducing a mood of agreeable melancholy. Earth seemed a place of exile, and I could dream of heaven. How quickly the afternoon was over and we had to go back to Les Buissonnets! But first I'd got to finish the food I'd brought with me in my basket; those jam sandwiches you [Pauline] cut for me, the bright contrast of their colours all faded, now, into a dull pink — no, this world was a depressing place, and there was to be no unclouded happiness this side of heaven.[2]

Everything grows old. In a sense what St. Thérèse of Lisieux was mourning was her own mortality. The child in all of us hungers for a world that is ever young. The mind does not breathe freely, cannot live its proper life in the atmosphere of the transitory and corruptible. It seeks another existence by which to exist itself. It is only by attaching itself to this, by wedding this indissolubly that it attains real existence. This universal experience of humankind lies at the heart of St. Thomas' ontological arguments for the existence of God. There is within us a concept of perfect being. But nothing on this earth completely satisfies us. "Our hearts are restless, Lord," as St. Augustine said, "until they rest in thee." We are surrounded by nothingness.

Some celebrated converts and Christians who are "reborn" falsify their Christian existence by disowning their past and affirming without reservation their present state of being. The annihilation of the part is true and authentic only in the context of the annihilation of the whole. This dawned on St. Paul gradually as he learned to see in his radical weakness the very ground of his strength. It is in the Gospels that man's nothingness is revealed as the unshakable, eternal ground of his love-relationship with the God Who Is.

Love is the great commandment, love of God and love of neighbor, a command that can only be an invitation. The condition of this love is humility, lowliness, all that tends to the full recognition of one's nothingness. So Jesus persuades his disciples to follow him because he is "meek and humble of heart" (Matt. 11:29). It is the theme of Mary's Magnificat (Luke 1:46-55), the theme of the beatitudes (Matt. 5:1-11), as well as most of the great parables. And what is very noticeable in the life of Christ is how he seems to enjoy the presence and expect the most of nobodies. Everything in his life centered on the love of his Father, and so he explored every dimension of man's nothingness, dereliction and annihilation, foreshadowed by the Old Testament. He who abases himself before the beloved is, in that very act of worship, self-obliviously exalted as a lover. On the level of being, reality and nothingness are contraries. But on the level of love they are reciprocal and equal partners. How would we ever appreciate fullness without emptiness, mercy without misery, being without nothingness? Our perceptive appreciation of the All depends essentially on how deeply we recognize our own nothingness.

Nothingness is not only the exclusive entrance into the mystic way; it is the only door into mental health and moral freedom. It is therefore regrettable that neither Freud nor Jung opened this door. Freud was a good scientist but a poor philosopher. Thanks to his friend and disciple Ernest Jones, who wrote a three-volume biography about him (*The Life and Works of Sigmund Freud*, 1961), we now know that Freud was also emotionally disturbed. Empirically he made a monumental contribution to our fund of knowledge regarding human nature. He was the first to understand the mystery, power and depth of the subconscious, and the first to assign adequate importance to the sexual impulse. But his knowledge of human nature was so specialized and limited and his followers so numerous and naive that at this point in history it seems quite probable that Freud did more harm than good.

In *The Future of an Illusion* (1927), Freud dismissed religion as an illusion based upon man's desire for a father figure. Wise men of the time objected that their religion was founded upon a feeling which they called "the oceanic feeling," using a phrase of Whitman's. By this they obviously meant a broad, overwhelming sense of *meaning*. Freud's extremely limited philosophical approach meant he had no phenomenology for dealing with such a notion. Philosophically speaking, his feet were firmly cemented into the "natural standpoint," the "triviality of everydayness."

What precisely can these people mean by "oceanic feeling," asks Freud. Adults have a sharp sense of their own limits which keeps them confined in a personal ego. Only babies—or the mentally ill—lack this clear dividing line. A baby is not consciously aware of where his own face ends and his mother's breast begins; it is all one warm, hazy cloud. Freud concludes triumphantly that we can explain this "oceanic feeling" as a throwback to early childhood, and see clearly that it has nothing to do with religion. Here one can see the essence of the reductionist method to solve a subtle problem by pretending it is, in fact, a crude and obvious one.

Freud's psychology is purely clinical, derived from the consulting room. It lacks what previous psychologies possessed: an account of the way we apprehend "meaning." Meaning is essentially what the Canadian theologian-philosopher Bernard Lonergan calls "insight." A Freudian psychology of mysticism is impossible because Freud's was an instinctual psychology. Instinct and spirit are incommensurable concepts. The question of whether or not a phenomenon is instinctual or spiritual is more important than whether it is conscious or unconscious. Why? Because, in contrast to the psychoanalytic concept, being human is not being driven but freely deciding what one is going to be. Being human is being existentially responsible for one's own existence.

Freud betrayed the self when he surrendered it to the *id;* and he denigrated the unconscious by limiting it to the instinctual. The person *is* spiritual and *has* a psychophysical overlay. Because he is spiritual at the core, a human being can become individualized and integrated.

It was the recognition of this fact that forced Carl Jung to part with his master, Sigmund Freud. Though Jung was not a God-centered man,—indeed he had no faith,—he did have a keen sense of "religion":

> Among all my patients in the second half of life—that is to say, over thirty-five—there has not been one whose problem in the last resort was not that of finding a religious outlook on life. It is safe to say that every one of them fell ill because he had lost that which the living religions of every age have given to their followers, and none of them has been really healed who did not regain his religious outlook.[3]

But Jung did not achieve a genuine unifying synthesis. He should have relied on Aristotelian phenomenology. Jung can be criticized for many reasons, but underlying all complaints against him is one fundamental inconsistency: upon a realistic view of the subjective and objective worlds as two independent realities mutually influencing each other, he superimposes the Kantian belief that we are unable to know anything at all about the objective world. Jung escapes Freud's sexual reductionism and falls into Kant's theoretical agnosticism. Jung does not say that man invents God; but neither does God exist objectively in and by himself. He is the personification of psychic forces.

Jung's "God" is a convenient abstraction covering all the different ideas of deity that have ever occurred in mankind's checkered history. Jung is not interested in God as an ontological reality but only the repercussions of this archetype in the human psyche. And so he prefers to use the technical word "self" rather than the ambiguous word "God."

God is for Jung an archetype, i.e., a type in the psyche. The word "type" is derived from the Greek "typos" meaning "imprint." Although Jung says that an imprint presupposes an imprinter, as a psychologist he is concerned with the *typos*, the imprint, a "symbol of an unknown and imcomprehensible content." Jung assiduously avoided confrontation with the unknown and referred to it insularly as "the religious point of view," lumping metaphysics, theology and faith under the same peculiar category.

From 1935 on Jung grew more and more aware of the centrality of religion in Western culture and in the psychic development of the human person. But the recognition of the value of the "imprint" evoked no personal belief in or religious response to the imprinter. Jung's faithlessness could not have been due to a lack of grace. This was an explanation to which he himself often resorted. But such a position is theologically untenable. Grace is indeed a gift, but one that is gratuitously and divinely bestowed on everyone.

A more likely reason for Jung's practical atheism—though he never denied God—was the unbending nature of his scientific mind, his single view which made any kind of faith whatever unacceptable. Carl Jung tried hard to escape from Freudian psychologism wherein religion is regarded as nothing more than a sublimation of an instinct. This was obviously a successful effort. He was, it seems, less successful in escaping from his own far more subtle version of psychologism or psychoidolatry, wherein God is nothing more than a psychic reality even though, as Jung says, this reality is irreducible.

Strictly speaking, Jung was not an atheist, not even an agnostic. He was an empirical investigator and allowed or forced both himself and his work to suffer enormously from the narrow confines of a rigid empiricism. Despite his rapacious desire to understand everything and the brilliant mind with which to do just that, he failed. And he failed precisely because he did not believe. He did not embrace the All. He could not adore.

In a recent life of Jung, (*C. G. Jung: The Haunted Prophet*, 1976), Dr. Paul Stern points out how many psychological difficulties Jung had to cope with in himself, how he was not always very successful, and how damaging the effects sometimes were. Despite this, his contribution was prodigious. But if I had to choose between Jung and Freud as a spiritual guide, I would choose Freud. I am not alone. According to Augustine Léonard O.P., "In comparison and because his method is so strict, Freud is less dangerous [from the religious point of view]. That which Jung calls religion, that which he honestly believes to be religion, is not religion at all; *even from the empirical point of view.* It appears to be only a very incidental manifestation."

Jung's inspired achievements suggest that, like Columbus, he discovered a continent without realizing what he had found. Columbus thought he had reached the Indies. Whenever Jung refers to the numinous archetype, which in "fear and trembling" discloses the *mysterium tremendum* in the depths of the soul, he always concludes with the somewhat embarrassed modesty of modern scientists who will tell us that only verifiable data are the objects of science. Jung can prove the "fear and trembling" which man exhibits when confronted with mystery. But fear and trembling of what? The answer, says Jung, does not concern science. Thus the most acute psychologist of our time is as helpless on the borders of the newly discovered continent as any other son of this scientific age.

Both Freud and Jung were bogged down by empiricism. From that limited standpoint there was no way they could enjoy insight into the meaning of nothingness. It seems to me that we have taken Freud and Jung too seriously. They were not the free men, nor were they the liberators we thought they were. If only we would take Christ, the psychologist par excellence, the perfect liberator, that seriously! He is the one who frees us from everything except love. Christ himself was the perfectly live man. He summoned every man to the same kind of freedom, the same perfection of love: "You must be made perfect as your heavenly Father is perfect" (Matt. 5:48). He points out in unmistakable terms the salient features of the *individuation process,* describing in detail both the dangers encountered and the means by which man and societies may become whole. The early Christian diagnosis of man makes comparable psychological attempts seem like a very weak cup of tea indeed. The discoveries of analytical psychology do little else than repeat, in modern phraseology, and with detailed empirical evidence, the principal injunctions of the Christian way.

Above all, Jesus preached the deep center, man's truest self, that something indestructible in the depths that never gives way, the kingdom of heaven within a man. It is the smallest of all seeds which will become the greatest of all herbs, a tree. It is the leaven that works upon and transforms the lump. It is the treasure hidden in a field, the pearl of great price, for which a man gives all. It is the bridegroom who comes when least expected, for whom unremitting watch must be kept. It is the narrow way which few discover, the straight gate by which a man finds his way to God.

The Denial of Death

Insight into our own nothingness prepares us for death. Death reduces a man to nothing and is only tolerable if he has already faced and accepted his nothingness. But, as usual, such a peaceful contemplation of death depends upon a prior vision: the vision of ultimate reality. The empiricist mind, the calculative intellect, is completely incapable of this vision.

Love transfigures death. Lovers of God such as Sts. Teresa of Avila and John of the Cross looked forward to death, almost pined for it. They knew it was the final breakthrough in the passionate pilgrimage toward the Absolute. "When I am away from Thee,/ What is my life to me?/ the agony of death./ None greater have I seen./ O, wretched that I am!/ For thus I persevere;/ I die because I do not die," wrote John in stanza three of his "A Soul Longing for the Vision of God."

Until we face death and embrace its terror, life escapes us and we are driven into all sorts of neurotic behavior and into (at least) hidden psychoses (character traits). At the heart of all our psychopathological tendencies and our defense mechanisms lies not sexual repression but *life-failure*. The fear of life and death paralyzes us. We repress globally until we find an acceptable, common form of partial paralysis, a pseudo-sanity approved by the mediocre masses of adult men and women.

In his later years Freud came to realize that what really bothers the child is the primary awesomeness of the external world, not so much his own inner drives. He spoke less of the Oedipus complex and more about "man's perplexity and helplessness in the face of [nature's] dreaded forces... the terrors of nature .. the painful riddle of death ... and the great necessities of Fate against which there is no help."[4] When it came to the central problem of anxiety, he no longer spoke of the child's being overwhelmed from within by his instinctual urges; instead, Freud's formulations became existential. Anxiety was now perceived as a reaction to global helplessness, abandonment and fate. Recent psychological developments have broadened even these perspectives. Now we know what really bothers the child: the devastating demands of life, with death lurking in the shadows, leering out from the heart of every life situation.

The whole character structure that we have developed and come to identify with ourselves has been put together under pressure of the social conventions to which we repressively adhere, not under pressure of the Spirit of God by whom we are freely led. What we've got to do therefore is die and be reborn long before we leave a corpse behind us. This is not easy to do. And it is not easy precisely because so much of us has to die.

Great writers such as C.S. Lewis and great psychologists such as Fritz Perls have conceived the neurotic structure as a thick edifice built up of many layers. These layers have got to be peeled off. From their sketches of the complex rings of defense that compose our character, our neurotic shield that protects our pulsating vitality from the awe-ful dread of truth, we can get some idea of the difficult and excruciatingly painful, all-or-nothing process that psychological rebirth is. And when it is through psychologically, it only begins humanly; the worst is not the death, but the rebirth itself.

In Chapter VII of his Narnian Chronicle entilted *The Voyage of the Dawn Treader*, C.S. Lewis provides us with a poignant portrayal of this as his character Eustace becomes "un-dragoned":

> I started scratching myself and my scales began coming off all over the place. And then I scratched a little deeper and, instead of just scales coming off here and there, my whole skin started peeling off.... Well,

exactly the same thing happened again. And I
thought to myself, oh dear, how ever many skins have
I got to take off?... The very first tear [the lion]
made was so deep that I thought it had gone right
into my heart. And when he began pulling the skin
off, it hurt worse than anything I've ever felt.[5]

What does it mean to be "born again"? Ernest Becker answers
that question superbly:

It means *for the first time to be subjected* to the terrifying paradox of the human condition, since one must
be born not as a god, but as a man, or as a god-
worm.... Only this time without the neurotic shield
that hides the full ambiguity of one's life. And so we
know that every authentic rebirth is a real ejection
from paradise, as the lives of Tolstoy, Péguy and others attest. It takes men of granite, men who were au-
tomatically powerful, "secure in their drivenness,"
and we might say it makes them tremble, makes them
cry—as Péguy stood on the platforms of Parisian bus-
ses with hot tears rolling down his cheeks while he
mumbled prayers.

Only after the asceticism that leads to death and the mysticism
that leads to rebirth are we ready for the final adventure of
death that, if done affirmatively, leads to heaven. Heaven is the
happy experience of a self so totally free that it is wholly immersed in the praise of God and the enjoyment of his Kingdom.

In death man becomes capable of his first completely personal
act; hence at death man is most disposed to respond to the divine
summons, to achieve his vocation and his destiny with the total
affirmation of his whole being. In that undivided and undis-
tracted moment man encounters Christ completely and with all
his being says "yes" to the sovereign claim of God, to all the

exigencies of love. The opportunity occurs not after death, when our eternal destiny is already fixed, nor before death in the debilitating state of dying; *but in death.*

In that moment when the soul leaves the body (not really the body but the corpse), it awakes suddenly to its pure spirituality and reaches the complete unity of its being. Then the person is free to decide for Christ or against him. Death, then, is rebirth. All roles are shed, and man, liberated in death, stands in his naked essence, his authentic self, before God without postponement, subterfuge, or escape. Ladislaus Boros describes this:

> Here—in death—God has completely overtaken man. By taking death on himself, he has closed up all ways of escape. Man has to go through death. And in death he will meet Christ irrecusably. Here the terrible adventure into which man has thrown himself—the adventure of keeping at a distance from God—comes to its end. Christ is now standing there, before man in death: clearly seen, luminously perceived, he calls man to himself with the gesture of redeeming love. Christ will for ever stand there, his love calling and seeking to give itself. If man in death decides against Christ, it makes no difference to Christ's love. But this love will burn him eternally, because he eternally experiences it as utterly close and nevertheless rejects it (and this is hell). But if he decides for Christ, then the same love of Christ becomes for him eternal light and final perfection in infinite happiness, the eternal acceptance of the closeness of our Lord (heaven). Thus the decision in the moment of death is the judgment itself.[7]

Man desperately wants to live. But he cannot face life without facing death—and he refuses, becoming sick and neurotic. Instead of suffering life to the point of death, he sublimates in sophisticated fashion and keeps death, and therefore new life, at a distance. He talks about life and analyzes it but doesn't live because he cannot endure the deaths it takes to come magnificently alive. He avoids the parlous adventure of life, the shame of the cross, and the ineluctable fact of death in every genuine "I-Thou" relationship, in every soulful act of love. He keeps "cuddling up" to persons and institutions, escaping the reality of death in cozy little huddles: in cliques, crowds, and seminars, in comfortable churches, petrifying prayer groups, and massive religious crusades.

If we don't face death and in Christ overcome it, we are still bound to sin. There is only one gateway to freedom and openness to the Ultimate, to infinite possibilities or finite impossibilities; that gateway is death. There is no new life without death of the old. The Christ-event brought the old world to a screaming halt. Sin is the intrusion of the old world imperatives and alternatives into the newness and loveness of the kingdom of God. The sinner acts as if the Christ-event never happened. We are all sinners. That is why we appear to be in a post-Christian era when, actually, we are still in a pre–Christian phase of evolution. We haven't taken Christ seriously yet. We have hardly begun to grasp his message and penetrate his mystery.

Unless we follow Christ into death—the death of the empirical separative ego and the ego's world—we prolong the "world" Jesus condemned, and we continue, despite some good efforts, to create an atmosphere of sin. We pollute the world with the pretty poison of make-believe pseudo-events and ersatz pleasures.

Death, as the ultimate breakthrough of our life, must involve a kind of violence—a wild human passion—if our proud self-imprisonment is to be broken open. The mystic prepares for the final act of death which will usher him into eternal life by striking mortal blows now to his false self, his grasping, craving ego.

Encountering death isn't the same as being in the danger of

death. Having a rope around your neck may not be as salvific as watching a leaf fall from a tree in autumn or burning a letter from your lover or selling your motorcycle.

No person or tradition has ever come up with a better way of dying, or defeating the ego, than the practice of poverty, chastity and obedience, which involve not principles of opposition to evil but expressions of a higher choice. The dynamic interplay of these virtues may be better understood if we translate these almost hackneyed words into their simplest and deepest meaning. Poverty means *no fuss.* Chastity means *no lust.* Obedience means *no rust.*

The *poor* man takes God so seriously that he takes everything else lightheartedly. He is drawn and captivated by Christ into the depths of reality where he cannot possibly trifle. He loses himself in the mystery of God. He becomes a champion of the rights of God and forgets all about his own problems. He takes good care of God's world and holds nothing cheap. It is his detachment from things that enables him to be a great lover of God and his whole creation.

The *chaste* man is at least as sexual and ardent as anyone. He doesn't grab or yearn to possess. He lets the people he loves go free and he becomes more and more liberated himself. He has learned to see and pass on. He is a one-joy man, wanting everything all at once, i.e., God, in the eternal now, and nothing apart from or less than that. He can only rest in God. But God, especially, is too good to be used. What does he do with God? He celebrates. A sexual symbolic celebration won't do. There is the Eucharist. And the prayer of ecstasy.

The *obedient* man does not subserviently do someone else's will. He is so acutely alive to all possible disclosures of the divine will that no *rust* could ever accumulate on his perceptive powers. *Oboedire* means "to listen." The obedient man is a good listener. From all eternity, says John of the Cross, God speaks one word, and that word reaches its fullness in Christ. The obedient man listens to the word with all his might all of the time. He absorbs, assimilates and digests it, becoming the word himself. He listens so intently that he is, like Christ, "obedient unto death, even to death on a cross" (Phil. 2:8).

The opposite of listening is not listening, or deafness. The Latin word is *absurdus*. If we are not obedient, we are absurd. The existentialists err when they cavalierly consider the world absurd; they are absurd themselves because they have not learned to listen with their whole being to the word, as T.S. Eliot says, listening so deeply that they become the music while the music lasts.

Donald Amireault, a Nova Scotia priest, once told me, "We all have two ears and one mouth because we're meant to listen twice as hard." This is what St. Benedict meant when he said we must listen "with the ear of the heart" (Prologue to the *Rule*). When we hear the word in our hearts, it "sends us." That's the meaning of the word "vocation" and of the word "apostle."

God does not speak in a vacuum or pull vocations out of hats. We need an abbot or a guru. Obedience means loving listening to another—to all the others—for the sake of the Wholly Other. Virtuous obedience is diametrically opposed to the regimentation of military obedience. It is an artful discipline.

The word "discipline" derives from the same root as the word "disciple," the student who lovingly listens to his teacher. The word "pupil" is similar. It means a little black thing in the eye, or a little child in school. Why is the same word used for both? Because the pupil looks into the eyes of the teacher and beholds the reflection of himself. The pupil is the intent looker, seeker, and listener, who absorbs the spirit of the teacher, and does what the teacher wants even before the teacher opens his mouth. *Pupila* means "little doll." What you see in the eyes of the teacher is a little doll that must become a mature, full-fledged, free person. That requires a great deal of trust. St. Benedict said that obedience must be "*sine murmuratione.*" There's no good translation for *murmuratione,* but it means basically, we must obey without grumbling. In other words, there's a close connection between stillness, silence and obedience. They must always go together. Through poverty, chastity and obedience, the mystic dies daily. Death strips man of all external possessions; the mystic anticipates this stripping by being content with the bare necessities of life (poverty). Death deprives man of his biological vitality; the celibate mystic freely fasts and deprives himself of sexual intercourse (chastity). Death means the end of man's pretended independence; the mystic sheds such a pretense by depending on the Church, or more specifically, on a spiritual director (obedience).

By choosing death now, freely and deliberately, letting it come when it may, he draws from that confrontation radical consequences for life really lived, creatively, exuberantly, divinely.

The Nothingness Neurosis

Whenever we deny our death and repress our sense of nothingness, we are plagued by what I call the nothingness neurosis, similar to Viktor Frankl's existential vacuum.

As human beings we are multiple amphibians, meant to be at home in many worlds, particularly the world of meaning. If we are deprived of the world of pure meaning, we are thrust inevitably into an intolerable form of life-failure, the root cause of our pathological behavior. Meaning stimulates the will, fills us with the desire to reach out to new horizons. It is meaning in the approaching person or in the sound of music that makes my heart leap. The more meaning I perceive the more vitality I experience. The peak experience is a sudden surge of meaning.

Our big problem is the meaninglessness and boredom of human life, the strange human incapacity to lay hold of experience, summarized in the nursery tale of an old woman who lived in a vinegar bottle. A passing fairy heard the old woman complaining about her unhappy lot, and obligingly transformed the vinegar bottle into a pretty cottage. Passing by again sometime later, the fairy stopped to see how the old lady was enjoying life, and again found her complaining—that the cottage was too damp and too small. The fairy changed the cottage into a small house. A month later, passing the spot, she heard the old woman complaining—she needed servants. The fairy changed the house into a palace. A few months later, the old woman was still as dissatisfied as ever—the place was too big, too cold, the servants slovenly. This time the fairy lost her patience and changed the palace back into a vinegar bottle.

If an alien intelligence from another solar system observed human beings in the face of death, he would probably conclude that men love life above all else, and that anything that increases the pleasure of life is good. He would therefore be somewhat baffled to see a play by Samuel Beckett, or to study the suicide-rate statistics in any large city. If men love life with such intensity, how can they treat it with such indifference, if they have no cause for complaint?

Creatures with strong negative impulses should have equally strong positive ones. The power of our denial of death should indicate a profound sense of purpose and an equally powerful appreciation of life. Yet our lives are wasted in trivialities. We are like spoiled children who kick and scream when they are told it is time to go to school, and yet are bored and bitter at home.

Boredom cripples the will. There is a threshold of the mind that can be stimulated by pain or inconvenience, but not pleasure. Colin Wilson calls this the "indifference threshold." If the will lies dormant for long periods of time, life fails. If the mind is going to focus on value, it needs to be exercised. What is required is daily mental discipline—or crises. A few decades ago the Greek poet Demetrios Capetanakis wrote:

> "Well," I thought when the war started, trying to hope for the best, "it will be horrible, but if it will be so

horrible as to frighten and wake up the mind, it will be the salavation of many. *Many are going to die, but those who are going to survive will have a real life, with the mind awake....*" But I was mistaken.... the war is frightening, but it is not frightening enough.[8]

Graham Greene, the great English novelist, tells us that in his teens life became meaningless for him and he sank into a condition of extreme boredom and depression. He found a way out by playing Russian roulette with his brother's revolver. When he pulled the trigger and did not die, he was overwhelmed by a feeling of delight, and a sense of the meaningfulness of life. Through a character called the Moviegoer, Catholic novelist Walker Percy describes a similar experience:

> Good as it is, my old place is used up (places get used up by rotatory and repetitious use) and when I awake, I awake in the grips of everydayness. Everydayness is the enemy. No search is possible. Perhaps there was a time when everydayness was not too strong and one could break its grip by brute strength. Now nothing breaks it—but disaster. Only once in my life was the grip of everydayness broken: when I lay bleeding in a ditch.[9]

Do we need to resort to such drastic measures? No. Meaning depends upon the mind's power of focusing, and focusing is a muscle that can be strengthened like any other muscle. Whatever enables me to concentrate my attention will do. If all perception is intentional, a reaching out, a focusing, on the part of the perceiver, then it ought to be possible to reconstruct any reality by making the necessary focusing effort.

If life drags on, the will gets run down. It will take a glorious holiday, or something like it, to remind us of wider meanings. Then suddenly we are enjoying everything more: eating, reading, walking, listening to music. The meaning sharpens the appetite for life—that is, the will to live. And the deeper my sense of the meaningfulness of the world, the fiercer and more persistent my will. Increased effort of will leads in turn to increased sense of meaning.

The mind's capacity to reach out for meaning is incalculable. This is marvelously illustrated in a story told by Romain Gary in his novel *The Roots of Heaven*. In a German concentration camp during the war, some French prisoners are becoming seriously depressed and demoralized. A man named Robert devises a way to arrest the decline. He suggests that they imagine an invisible girl sharing their prison quarters. If one of them swears, he must bow and apologize to the "girl." When they undress they must hide behind a blanket. The game works; morale is restored. The commandant orders them to hand over the "girl." They refuse. Robert is arrested and put into solitary confinement. He survives by reaching out again to other realities by the power of his imagination and sees before him great herds of elephants trampling over endless plains.

By a series of self-images we can come to enjoy deeper states of self-awareness or what Colin Wilson calls "promotion" of the personality. The self-image provides me with a kind of artificial standard of objective values. It gives me a sense of external meaning. If I allow the will to become passive and the senses to close up, the meaning of life will escape me. If I want more meaning, I must force my senses wide open by an increased effort of will. This is no time for the mortification of the senses. That comes later when they have done their utmost to fill the mind with meaning, and can do no more.

We might think of the senses as spring-loaded shutters that must be forced open, and which close again when you let them go. If I let these shutters close too soon I lose my objective values and succumb to podsnappery. It will then take some spectacularly stunning event to snap me out of my subjective, cloistered world. If I get myself into a snit over some trivial matter and then hear about some old friend in dire straits, I instantly snap out of my black mood, for my emotions are cut down to their proper size by comparison with a more serious reality. Moods and emotions are a kind of fever produced by a lack of contact with reality. What sustains the scientist as well as the poet and the mystic is an increasing sense of contact with reality.

Sedentary philosophers—David Hume of the eighteenth century, for example—fail to notice the importance of the will because thinking uses so little of it. Put one of these fellows on a motorcycle in the heart of Boston or Los Angeles and he will become acutely aware of the reality of his will and freedom of choice! His wholly activated self will be in command, for a man involved in such dangerous activity, requiring split-second timing, is aware of dozens of choices he can make—overtaking, breaking, cutting-in, accelerating. Making the right choice at the right time is a matter of life or death.

Most of us let the robot take over most of the time. We must admit that, for ninety-nine percent of our lives, we remain in a state of psychic numbness resembling the automatized condition of the lobotomized pigeon. What Sartre said about his café proprietor in *Nausea* could apply to us all: "When his café empties, his head empties too." Our mental pressure sinks like a tire with a puncture. And it will contrive to sink unless we find the "moral equivalent of war." That's what Christianity is: a way of life that is dissatisfied with the constricted vision of the average person. Colin Wilson summarizes this well:

> There is something *wrong* with "normal" human consciousness. For some odd reason, we seldom get the best out of it. The main trouble seems to lie with our sense of values, which only seems to come alive in moments of great excitement or crisis. Otherwise it snores hoggishly, and we only live at half-pressure. The trouble seems to lie in the co-operation of the conscious and subconscious mind. If you keep up a

certain conscious straining, you will "let loose subconscious allies behind the scenes"; this happens most notably in religious experience. We are certainly capable of a far broader and deeper sense of reality than the one we are accustomed to. The fascinating area, for psychology, lies in this realm of "values"; and this in turn seems to be a matter of the collaboration of the conscious and subconscious parts of the mind—a collaboration that, ideally, would be *directed* by the conscious mind and *powered* by the subconscious. The conscious mind must learn to understand the subconscious—not only to call its bluff when it shams fatigue, but how to make the best possible creative use out of it.[10]

Later on in the same work, Wilson gets to the very heart of the human condition when he analyzes *spoiltness* in penetrating, phenomenological terms. He defines spoiltness as:

the limit beyond which an individual refuses to make an effort without *immediate returns.* The spoilt child demands a very high level of rewards and petting from life. But our limits also depend upon how *far* we can see, upon how far-sighted our purposes are. And this brings us up against the basic evolutionary problem of mankind: our *short-sightedness.* [italics mine]. This is the real significance of spoiltness; it is nothing less than the human condition itself, another name for "original sin." Kierkegaard saw that the basic problem is that *all men are bored.* First Adam was bored to be alone, so Eve was created; then Adam and Eve were bored, so they had Cain and Abel; then all the family was bored, so Cain killed Abel. . . . Human history is seen as a flight from boredom, and from the low mental pressure associated with it. But boredom is another expression of spoiltness; it is a refusal to make any mental effort without the reward of an external stimulus.[11]

The healthy person is the one who wills to live no matter what. The integrated person is the one who wills to live fully and use the imaginative initiative required. Otto Rank, the last of Freud's major disciples to break away and follow his own path, makes a revolutionary assertion: The real benefit that a patient derives from being psychoanalyzed is that the clash with the psychoanalyst revives his deflated and passive will.

Because of recent Oriental influences and our own peculiar penchant for *instant* achievement, we tend to become too passive too soon, skipping steps along the way. There are active steps toward the supernal end which are unskippable. In order to see anything—*really* see it—we have to do half the work; we have to reach out and switch on our meaning perception. If this muscle is left slack, it produces the sensation that Sartre calls "nausea," in which the world appears meaningless. If it is exercised and becomes very strong, the result is mystical intensity.

Neurosis—distinct from the strain and tension of the healthy personality—is essentially a passive state. That is why psychologists such as Viktor Frankl and Abraham Maslow talk about self-transcendence and self-actualization when they concentrate on the evolution of healthy individuals. Everybody is potentially a self-actualizer. It depends mostly on free will and courage, not on circumstances. Maslow's "hierarchy-of-values" theory insists that our transcendent urges—aesthetic, creative, religious—are as basic and permanent a part of human nature as dominance or sexuality. If they are less obviously universal, this is only because fewer human beings reach the point at which they take over.

Ludwig Binswanger, Erwin Straus and Medard Boss have made a tremendous contribution to existential psychology. Like Martin Heidegger, they have been mainly concerned to analyze the various forms of "inauthentic existence" into which man is trapped by the triviality inherent in civilized life. While other psychologists were thinking in terms of sexual repression, they recognized that various "compulsive neuroses" represented a kind of blockage of the vital system.

The mind, like the body, must be considered as a whole; in order to stay healthy, it must be exercised as a whole. The mentally healthy individual is the one who habitually calls upon deep levels of vital reserves. An individual whose mind is allowed to become dormant—so that only the surface is disturbed—begins to suffer from circulation problems. Neurosis is the feeling of being cut off from my own powers. But when I am in an active, healthy state of mind, unexpected pleasures—serendipities—are always producing at least minor peak experiences. The peak experience, with its sense of objective meaning worth striving toward, releases my vital reserves. I thus have plenty of reasons for making effort, and it is through effort that the will stays healthy.

Graham Greene wrote a powerful novel entitled *The Power and the Glory,* in which his "whiskey priest," about to be executed by a firing squad, feels suddenly that it would have been easy to be a saint. Throughout the novel he is weak, listless and sinful. The robot controlled most of his living activities. But when he stands there looking into the barrels of five loaded rifles, he perceives that his weakness and misery are nothing more than hypochondria; they vanish like nightmares. A few hours ago he walked across the courtyard and it hardly seemed real; nothing he saw mattered very much. Why? Because he had long ago surrendered the driver's seat. If his execution were delayed and he could now walk back across that same courtyard, he would do so with wide-eyed wonder and radical astonishment. Puddles would seem like oceans, soldiers like gods. With his robot suppressed, he would see everything directly with his own eyes and live in masterful harmony with his own human instrument and his whole environment.

Automatized living produces a state of *imprisonment*. In the face of death the "whiskey priest" became suddenly and dramatically de-automatized. Meditation, along with a recollected style of life is meant to produce the same effect long before death. Without daily meditation and habitual recollection, the robot takes over, and all the adventurous possibilities of human existence are lost forever. What this amounts to is mental suffocation in a world without newness, and what it ends up as is permanent life-failure.

In his most recent novel, Walker Percy attacks the life-failure that has become our American way of life. Playing Jeremiah to Hugh Hefner and his entourage, Percy is a voice crying out in a wilderness of porno shops and massage parlors. Although not enthralling as a whole, *Lancelot* includes some significant insights. Speaking through his madman, Percy is positively eloquent in his rage:

> I cannot tolerate this age. And I will not. I might have tolerated you and your Catholic Church [speaking to the priest], if you had remained true to yourself. Now you're part of the age. You've the same fleas as the dogs you've lain down with. I would have felt at home at Mont-Saint-Michel, the Mount of the Archangel with the flaming sword, or with Richard Coeur de Lion at Acre. They believed in a God who said he came not to bring peace but the sword. Make love not war? I'll take war rather than what this age calls love. Which is a better world, this... fornicating Happyland U.S.A. or a Roman legion under Marcus Aurelius Antonius? Which is worse, to die with T.J. Jackson at Chancellorsville or live with Johnny Carson in Burbank?[12]

Percy condemns the "nothingness neurosis" that characterizes our age. The opposite of this psychasthenic condition is the self-transcendence of the man with a mystical mind, the man who

lives under such divine inner pressure—not nervous tension—
that he is always tapping inner reserves, climbing into higher
states of consciousness, and seeing the connections between everything. The enjoyment of this mystical vision, the perceptive
appreciation of the inner suchness of things, leading as it does to
the intensity and universality of love—this is the mystical life.
The hunger and thirst we all have for more and more of this life
is what underlies all our other human drives. It was to lead us
into the fullness of Christian vitality that Jesus came into the
world: "I came that [you] may have life and have it more abundantly" (John 10:10).

Notes

[1]St. Teresa of Avila, *The Interior Castle*, p. 244.

[2]*Autobiography of St. Thérèse of Lisieux*, translated by Ronald Knox
(New York: Kenedy, 1958), p. 28.

[3]Carl Jung, *Modern Man in Search of a Soul*, translated by W. S. Dell
and Carl F. Baynes (New York: Harcourt Brace, 1933), p. 229.

[4]Sigmund Freud, *The Future of an Illusion* (New York: Doubleday An-
chor Books, 1964), pp. 31, 24, 21, 82.

[5]C. S. Lewis, *The Voyage of the Dawn Treader* (New York: Macmillan,
1952), pp. 88, 89.

[6]Ernest Becker, *The Denial of Death* (New York: The Free Press,
1973), p. 58.

[7]Ladislaus Boros, *Pain and Providence* translated by Edward Quinn
(Baltimore: Helicon, 1966), pp. 95-96.

[8]Quoted in Colin Wilson, *New Pathways in Psychology* (New York: Tap-
linger, 1972), p. 28.

[9]Walker Percy, *The Moviegoer* (New York: Alfred A Knofp, (1962), p.
145.

[10]Colin Wilson, *New Pathways in Psychology*, p. 87.

[11]*Ibid.*, pp. 104-105.

[12]Walker Percy, *Lancelot* (Farrar, Straus and Giroux, 1977), pp. 157-
158.

Part III: Celebration

.

Chapter 5
Christian Vitality

When we can say with St. Paul, "It is no longer I who live, but Christ lives in me" (Gal. 2:20), then we know what mysticism is. We are graced with such amazing Christian vitality that we are transformed into Christ. Through, with, and in him we enjoy realized union with God.

Awakened in Faith

As St. John of the Cross said: "The only proximate and immediate means of union with God is faith." The mature Christian allows God to wean him away from all the baby food of the spiritual life—all sense-based knowledge—so that he will be able to live by faith alone. We must become detached from all that is not God, if we are to become attached to God himself.

To live by faith is to go in one direction. When the disciples could not cure the epileptic boy, Christ exclaimed: "O faithless and *perverse* generation" (Matt. 17:16). These words throw light on the meaning of faith. There is an interesting connection between the two adjectives. In the Greek the meaning of the word translated as "perverse" signifies "turning in many directions." In other words, to be without faith is to act convulsively. So a faithless man is perverse in this sense. Because of our lack of faith we are tyrannized by multiple, conflicting moods, and drawn into many directions all at once.

The Gospels speak mainly of a possible inner evolution called "rebirth." They are psychological documents delineating two things: first, the early Christian community's experience of a brand-new kind of man, Jesus Christ; second, the teachings of the *new man,* which if understood and followed, would lead to such an inner evolution that it would amount to a transformation into Christ. The psychology of mysticism is the psychology of man—the new man; in other words, a psychology of mysticism is, or ought to be, a coherent and dynamic teaching about the transformation of man.

The Passion and Ressurection of Christ empowered man to be reborn and become, not bigger, better, nicer, but *new.* The starting point of this re-creation is faith: the conviction, the certainty, that a deeper interpretation of life exists, and as a consequence, that wild Christian vitality is possible. Faith in essence is utterly different from what we usually call belief. Faith, in fact, undermines all our ordinary and natural beliefs because it leads *away* from worldly belief and in a direction that can no longer be confirmed by natural belief and the evidence of sense. Life as we know it through the senses is not the end, but the means to another end governed by faith.

We cannot understand the meaning of faith unless we appreciate the fact that man lives on several different levels. Man has not become his best self. His deepest levels are left unactivated. He needs to complete himself. That is what eros is for. Nothing external can complete him. What is deeper, more real, and more godly is *in him;* but it is as yet unknown, unactualized. The *new man*—the Christ—is hidden in everyone. The Gospels tell us about the burgeoning new Christ in every man.

The Greek word for faith—*pistis*—is from the verb *peitho* which means to persuade, or make to obey. What in man will make all sides of himself obey him? What is it in man that will compel every aspect and dimension of his humanity to yield its power to the pure essence of him, the deepest possibility of him? If man could find this secret he would be master of himself, not directly, through his own power, but through the power given him by faith.

Faith is rooted in the deepest domain of man far below the range of the senses. When our Lord chided his disciples for their lack of faith it was because they were merely impressed by Christ as an extraordinary man and miracle worker. And when Jesus said it was expedient that he leave them (John 16:7), this was because as long as he was among them, a visible body, they could not have faith and so could not really re-create themselves.

The order of truth belonging to the category of "faith" is entirely different from the order of truth belonging to the senses, provable by the senses. Nicodemus was told how useless it was to believe simply because of miracles (John 3:1-21). In fact, the visible miracles stood in his way. They could not touch that level of the mind that could only be awakened by faith.

In chapter seventeen of Luke, the disciples ask Christ to increase their faith, and he describes for them the basic attitude upon which faith depends for growth. He had already referred to it in the seventh chapter of Luke when he told the story of the centurion. He comes back to it again now: man must realize he is *under authority*. Faith is the certain realization of a deeper level of existence to which man must subject everything in him. A free man who lives by faith does not do whatever he wants but really wants to do what he *must* in order to be his best self. All the teachings of Christ are about this deeper level or this higher possible degree of man. This knowledge is not like the easily verified knowledge gained through visible life and the senses. It must be understood by the mind. This is faith. Everything else about man, every other aspect of him, is subjected to this faithful vision. He transcends himself. And in the end he does not boast of self-control. He says: "I am an unprofitable servant; I have done that which I ought to do" (cf. Luke 17:10).

When Christ went up onto the Mount of Transfiguration with three of his disciples he proved to them in some way—how, we do not know—that the transformation of man is a reality. The disciples could scarcely comprehend and not only were afraid but, as it says in one account, were so *asleep* that they could not perceive what was happening until they were brought into a full *waking state.* Luke says it clearly: "Peter and they that were with him were heavy with sleep. And waking, they saw his glory..." (Luke 9:32). The evangelist does not refer to ordinary sleep. After all it was daytime. He was talking about the partial mind, psychic numbness, letting the robot take over, while we live apathetically in the shallows.

When Jesus said: "Let the dead bury their dead" (Matt. 8:22), obviously he is not referring to people who are literally dead, but to people partially immersed in life who can see nothing save the interests of the world. In the same way people are divided into those who are asleep and those awake. "Wake up from your sleep," says St. Paul, "rise from the dead, and Christ will shine on you" (Eph. 5:14). We must rouse our dispersed spirit from its stupefied torpor and wake the sleeper in us.

Because the disciples were not fully awake, they were not open to the transformation of man and his world but in search of a Messiah, a national hero, an earthly kingdom. That is why from beginning to end, Jesus, the stranger from Galilee, remained an utterly mysterious person—like the cowboy who rides into town out of nowhere. Jesus was not—and could not possibly be— primarily the man for others, but rather, the man from the Other. We know almost nothing of his first thirty years. He spent this part of his life unknown, held and captivated by his Father, the holy ineffable, mysterious One. Even during his brief active period, his worldly career, he could not resist the pull and dynamism of his Father, the tug of his roots which lay in other worlds; and so he was compelled to seek silence and solitude in the desert, out on the water, up the mountain. He dwelt too long in sacred places such as the temple and had to say defensively: "Did you not know that I must be about my Father's business?" (Luke 2:49).

People then were like people today: personality seekers, celebrity hounds. They found Jesus to be a giant of a man, a new kind of man. They wanted to groove on him, feed off him—but remain in their good ruts unchanged. Jesus' style of life made that impossible. His personal vitality was contagious. We learn something important about the use of verbal instruments from the Word made flesh. The Word does not philosophize or theologize much at all. He makes acts of love, comforts, heals, inspires. His sparse words are personal, vocational, vital, challenging: come, follow, see, love, suffer, taste, change, become. He seems oblivious of definitions. He answers our questions not by correct formulations but by courageous action. What he *does* is his word. He *is* what he does. The infinite and ineffable God makes himself known not by becoming articulate but by becoming vitally present through action. The thing Christ started was active and lively enough to be called a march through history.

Jesus never catered to the crowds. He died ignominiously. When he rose from the dead in all his glory he was more unmanageable than ever—almost unrecognizable. Mary Magdalene thought he was the gardener (John 20:15). The disciples on the road to Emmaus thought him a stranger until he broke bread with them (Luke 24:30-32). After the Resurrection he lingered on the earth, in and out of his disciples' presence, just long enough to tend the flame he had come to ignite in their hearts so that they themselves, like him, would become Goddened, in their own human, earthy and worldly way. Then he vanished into the abyss and left them on their own. This is Western mysticism. You get haunting glimpses of it and you see it reenacted again and again in the best episodes of the Western cowboy movies.

The Celebration of Life

All man needs to survive is a little bread and water. But in order to avoid life-failure and enjoy real Christian vitality, he needs to celebrate the gift of his life and the whole of creation that makes life so livable.

The secret, the source, and the central expression of the mystical life is celebration. But most of us do not know how to celebrate because we have sacrificed ourselves to "civilization as we know it," which we presume to be the healthiest and best possible. We think we have the highest standard of living in the history of the world. I'm sure we have the lowest in the history of the planet because we do not know what it feels like to be alive.

The last half century of what we call civilization has almost ruined us. When the automobile appeared and threatened children's lives, youngsters were fenced into a restricted area of the backyard. When the recreational vehicle appeared, the crowded campsite off the side of the road became not only our backyard but everybody else's.

Backyards are no more conducive to vibrant human vitality than zoos are productive of normal animal behavior. We all need to express rather primitive, passionate patterns of living, even savage instincts and barbarian tendencies, mystic queries born of inherent otherworldliness. The backyard is no place for this. Neither is the city for that matter. In the open country—woods, fields, farms, lakesides—our backyard expands to include the whole world. In urban areas everything is owned and guarded except in the gutter. This is frustrating. A man's environment is not his own. Man is, in fact, a victim of his environment. He cannot climb these trees or cut these flowers or explore this territory. He is deprived of the natural and necessary process of adventure.

In the name of safety and sanity we discourage and eliminate activities which are essential to our full human life. We aim to protect ourselves from danger and from shock when normal living is fraught with immense and innumerable dangers. We barricade, supervise, and protect ourselves at every turn. So the country is full of baby pens, schoolyards, and yellow lines, signs growth—spiritual dwarfs, manikins. Even monasteries, the last bulwark in the world for great-souled men of bold and daring aspiration, are full of dead men, curbed and cornered, stymied and atrophied at every turn by rules devised not toward progressively enlightening the mind by putting on the mind of Christ, and enlarging the heart even to the compass of Christ's heart—which is the essence of sanctity; but contrived, rather, to eliminate all those aspects of life which involve challenge and risk, no matter how salvific and sanctifying and compelling.

This deplorable state of affairs exists because our civilization by its very nature kills the priceless and irreplaceable qualities of childhood: enthusiasm, originality, creativity and hope. In this sense it is true to say, that when you cease to be a child you are already dead. For all that is good and holy and enduring is built on the basic, underlying foundation of a child's lust for life.

Appalling and incredible as it seems to be, it is blatantly evident that there are legions of grown-up people who have been robbed of their childhood, deprived of the basic experiences of growing up. They have never been cut, bruised, skinned, lost or challenged. They have never seen a chicken killed or a kitten born; never slept in the woods or even on the porch; never stretched out on the green grass under the sun or climbed a cliff; never skated or skied; never planted a seed or raised a crop; never conversed with a dog or romped through the fields or rolled down a hill; never camped out by themselves or swum in the nude. They do not know the taste or the meaning of solitude, silence and adventure.

They have been introduced only vaguely and vicariously into the world of nature with its kaleidoscopic deployment of multifarious, mysterious life. They go boating but cannot swim. They have never seen farther than the natural span of the eye; never probed deeper than the bare fact, never penetrated deeper than the surface, never reached, even remotely, the most real world, the most exciting level of human life; the realm of supernature, of angels, saints, God, and the eternal immutable verities. They have never communed with God. We deny ourselves so many pleasures not only because they are unsafe, but because they are inconvenient or interfere with bedtime. Think of what we miss: the glory of the waxing or waning harvest moon; searching the shore at night for ghost crabs, those unusual looking beings rarely glimpsed in the daytime; the hooting of owls, nighthawks, and other nocturnal creatures; the ordinary splendor of stars, the dark night ablaze with silver jewels. (We ought to have such familiar kinship with the stars that we know them by name and miss them by day.) The memory of such ecstasies can more than make up for the loss of a few hours' sleep.

Those who have had the unfortunate experience of a truncated, effete childhood—for all their wonderful accomplishments, such as the atom bomb—are not really conscious, because they have had no true, primary experience of life and lead a derivative existence. Their vitality is thin, their feeling meager, their passion weak. They must rediscover their true needs, and insist that these needs are rights, and that these rights are being violated in a tenuous cellophane civilization.

Adult America's desire for fun and games in any form is the great symbol of misspent—or rather unspent—childhood. We are at the same time remarkably overdosed and underentertained, in spite of vast quantities of movies, games, sports, and other diversionary tactics. Entertainment is enfeebled precisely because it is available in such familiar capsules and we swallow it without tasting. It is possible that these copious draughts of pleasure would have supplied a need in childhood, but now they merely aggravate and befuddle.

May not the aggressive, hostile and irresponsible exploitation that characterizes the corporate world be a recrimination against the damage inflicted upon future businessmen in their childhood? Is the insanity of our population due to an inability to face the adult world or an inability to acknowledge the terrible destitution of a lost childhood?

We have a compelling and everlasting need to be not childish, but childlike. "Unless you be converted and become as little children, you shall not enter into the kingdom of heaven" (Matt. 18:3). The kingdom our Lord referred to is not some ethereal realm over against and apart from the concrete, human world we live in; it is the abundance of life made real and accessible, here and now, in the heat and turmoil of this world, to all those wise and willing enough to be childlike. And this infusion of new life comes directly from God who cannot resist the lure of a child.

The Meaning of Festivity

How do we recover a lost childhood? We can begin by wasting time creatively, by celebrating festively. We are, in fact, obliged to waste Sunday, engaged all day long in the highest, purest and most useless human activities—playing and praying. But we need to celebrate more than the sabbath.

Man is never more a man than when he celebrates festively—a capacity which lies right at the heart of human life, and perhaps constitutes it. How does he celebrate? First of all, by contemplation—a fact unrecognized by the crowd but long attested to by leaders in all traditions and ages—Plato, Aristotle, Buddha, Lao-Tzu, Thomas Aquinas, Aldous Huxley, Teilhard de Chardin, Suzuki (contemporary Japanese interpreter of Zen Buddhism to the West). Contemplation means living so keenly, in focus, in simplicity, that you reach the highest pitch of awareness, the most total kind of presence.

Complete, undivided presence is heaven, the opposite is hell. Whenever we celebrate, above all we celebrate presence—the presence of man, God, the world—not as means but as an end, the object of our love and praise. Whenever we succeed in bringing before our mind's eye the hidden ground of everything that is, we succeed to some degree in performing an act that is meaningful in itself, and have a "good time." In the act of contemplation we affirm the totality of being; we see and experience the presence of God. And this experience empowers us to live out our universal assent to the world as a whole.

Festivity is more than the mere absence of work. Leisure is more than our free time. Very few of us are capable of creative leisure, of true festivity, because we are driven by a neurotic compulsion to work in a utilitarian society that makes everything useful. By a despair from weakness, slothfulness of the heart, a man is driven out of his own house, his settlement or contentment, into the nitty-gritty of work, into endless, sophisticated chatter, into incessant entertainment by empty stimulants, into an inhuman arena of monumental trivia, where there is no room for the serenity and intensity of intrinsically meaningful activity, for contemplation, for festive celebration.

A cocktail hour during which a few friends are deeply and leisurely engaged can be a humanizing event only if it closes the door on the routine, utilitarian workaday world and leads into the contemplative and festive evening of family life where men, women, and children rediscover one another in leisure and love. A banquet meal helps, too, when real things—bread and wine, flowers and candles—lead us to affirm and be nourished by the reality of one another, with no attempt to manipulate or exploit. Best of all is the Eucharistic meal, both convivial and sacrificial, by which we focus on Christ and enter deeply and recklessly into the mystery of love, the mystery of God. (See next chapter, "Our Daily Bread," pp. 131-154.)

When we celebrate, we imitate God. We imitate the contemplation of his Seventh Day when he stopped working, took a long, loving look at the world and delighted in it. And he has never gotten this delight out of his system! The world is, because he likes it. Each one of us is, because he loves us. What cause for celebration!

The trick is not to arrange a festive event but to find people who can en-joy (put joy into) it. Joy, the fruit of festivity, is pure gift and cannot be organized, arranged or induced. It is the echo of God's presence. That is why God-centered men are always joyous and the classical man is always a grave-merry one. St. Francis de Sales said, "A sad saint is a sorry saint" And St. Teresa of Avila ardently pleaded, "Lord, deliver me from sour-faced saints!"

Only the saints can afford to be merry. They are so securely rooted in God and take him so seriously that they naturally tend to treat everything else lightheartedly. Ever hear a man on a tightrope laugh or tell a joke? Only a man who knows that God loves him can live in this world with a good sense of humor, a lively wit, and an abiding peace of soul.

Festivity must be more than memorial. According to Josef Pieper's work, *In Tune with the World,*

> Strictly speaking, the past cannot be celebrated fes-
> tively unless the celebrant community still draws glory
> and exaltation from that past, not merely as reflected
> history, but by virtue of a historical reality still opera-
> tive in the present. If the Incarnation of God is no
> longer understood as an event that directly concerns
> the present lives of men, it becomes impossible, even
> absurd to celebrate Christmas festively.[2]

The fine arts have kept alive the memory of true festivals when they began to wither and be forgotten in the Church. An essential part of any festivity is the artistic act: making music, reading poetry, dancing. These corybantics enable us to live full human lives. Notice how almost all the ethnic dances let certain limbs go limp. The head must not move, and no noise may be made with the feet. Something everywhere is always saying "no" as a hint to the "no-ness" that lies at the heart of delight, of festivity. No trespassing on the part of those workaday boots and cunning heads seared with fuss, bleared and smeared with toil—that is what the dance steps are telling us.

No man can live without pleasure. In the absence of towering, satisfying pleasure, he substitutes a paltry surrogate. Any of these events which exploit reality for utilitarian purposes is a pseudo-event and a sham. A sham production is worse than no festivity at all. It does not play in the lap of reality like a child with no other end except assent, love, and praise of creation.

Man became dehumanized when he lost his capacity for festivity. His failure to recognize this loss is even more catastrophic. Lao-Tzu said that a man isn't sick as long as sickness sickens him. How depressing to see the crowds mistake the commercialized folderol of Christmas for the genuine spirit of festivity! When we are unaware that sham festivals have replaced true festivity, our dehumanization is complete.

There can be no true celebration without sacrifice. Consider the turkey, which on Thanksgiving gives up being a mere turkey and becomes the men around the dinner table. Or Zorba, the Greek's live fish—those you see jumping out of the water—sacrificing the snug, safe security of the water for air, that awful human stuff. The principle of feast implies its polarity: the fast. So the penitential season of Advent precedes Christmas and Lent Easter. We must live festally, for life without occasions is not worth living, but ferially, too, for life is so much more than occasions.

A festivity is not merely a cheerful get-together. It erupts as we affirm the intrinsic goodness of existence in an act of love. And it may turn out that this goodness is never revealed to us so brightly and powerfully as by the sudden shock of loss and death. So tragedy can sometimes be a part of festivity. Sacrifice is always its soul. If we have no ferial experience, we cannot know the grandeur of festive celebration.

Man cannot make what is to be celebrated any more than he can make the rain. The festival is a day "the Lord has made" (Ps. 118:24). An entirely human institution cannot be a real festival. Pieper tells us:

> There can be no festivity when man, imagining himself self-sufficiant, refuses to recognize that Goodness of things which goes far beyond any conceivable utility; it is the Goodness of reality taken as a whole which validates all other particular goods and which man himself can never produce nor simply translate into social or individual "welfare." He truly receives it only when he accepts it as pure gift. The only fitting way to respond to such gift is: by praise of God in ritual worship. In short, it is the withholding of public worship that makes festivity wither at the root.[3]

Public worship then, good art, pure love, the Christian concept of sacrifice and death, a genuine philosophy and, above all, contemplation, can once again inspire in us that spirit of celebration which makes every man man-full.

Biblical Sensuousness

The mystical experience involves many levels of feeling differing in emphasis and quality and mediated by many different images and conceptions. Some of its more general forms comprise a feeling of oneness and cosmic unity, of wholeness and depth, an awesome sense of the holy, a feeling of absolute dependence, of ultimate rightness and an unspeakably wonderful sense of objectless joy. Religious feeling reaches its summit when it becomes love of a personal God. What makes this whole range of feeling essentially religious is that one is taken out of and beyond his ordinary self, out of and beyond the limited world in which he lives and is opened up to what is unlimited and unapprehensible, though felt as overwhelmingly real and joyful. It should be obvious that religious feeling has no object in the ordinary sense, but is directed toward mystery as its term of focus. In summing up this subject, Charles Davis says:

> What my analysis means, then, is that mystical experience is not something apart from ordinary religion, but the coming into explicit consciousness of the primary constitutive element of all genuine religion; namely, religious feeling understood as an immediate, spontaneous, connatural response to transcendent reality. In the mystic, the awareness of mystery becomes explicit, and this allows it to dominate consciousness, sometimes absorbing it completely.
> Thus true religion is rooted primarily in the affections. It is the deepest arousal of our affectivity. How is it, then, that religion, mystical religion particularly, has—with reason—been seen as the enemy of the body and the affections?[4]

Our inability to celebrate life with reckless abandon may be due in part to our traditional suspicion of the body—the weakest and most defective aspect of the Christian tradition and most other traditions as well. This defect in the West is diametrically opposed to the original and essential Christian teaching, and is strikingly at odds with the life of Christianity's earthy founder and his robust and ribald disciples.

We have been talking about mystical experience in terms of a total human response to mystery. We've got to remember now that this response is personal and *embodied.* We must therefore include our affectivity and acknowledge the processes of material mediation implied by our complex makeup as embodied persons.

Charles Davis introduces a helpful distinction between sensuousness and sensuality. We are sensuous, he says, when we participate in the spontaneous rhythms and responses of the body and are open to the joys and delights, the pain, suffering, and stress of bodily experience. Sensuousness implies relaxation, which frees the body from the driving impetus of the rational mind and will. Sensuality, in contrast, puts the body in rigid subjection to the mind and uses it as an instrument of pleasure for reasons found in man's mental and spiritual state. The roots of sensuality are not in bodily impulses, but in man's mind. John Wren-Lewis put it this way:

> The body itself seems to know that it does not want sensual indulgence. It takes only a small amount of real sensory awareness to awaken the body to the fact that it is being biologically maltreated by the way the mind organises life, and this maltreatment happens as much when the individual wallows in self-indulgent sensuality as it does when he strives neurotically for wealth and power, regiments himself to mechanical work-routines or suffers extreme poverty.[5]

Sensuality is the enslavement of the body to the domineering consciousness of a mind alienated from its bodiliness. The traditional version had it the other way around. I would further argue, with Davis, that sensuousness accompanies a sacramental, mystical view of the world, in which the body and physical nature are mediatory of the spirit, whereas sensuality implies a destruction of the mediatory, symbolic character of the physical world and the reduction of that world to mere physicality.

One of the people who caught the significance of this and shared it with the world in his own uniquely compelling way was the Jewish philosopher Martin Buber. He said that we must put our arms around the vexatious world; only then do our fingers reach the realm of lightening and grace. He believed that man was intended to enjoy to the full the created world. Though Buber denied himself self-sacrificingly and affirmed life fully, he avoided the two extremes of a masochistic unenlightened ascetism on the one hand, and a precious egotistic libertinism on the other. He did not attempt to conquer nature, subdue the flesh, or stifle the surging forces of life. Such rigidity produces nothing but harshness and severity. There was no opposite tendency in him to confuse liberty with license and freedom with impulse.

Roy Larson of the *Chicago Sun-Times* accuses the playboys and playmates of the Western world of "gulping, rather than sipping the wine of life . . . they desensitize their taste buds." Sensuous at first, "they become sensationalists in the end, incapable of responding to anything but the most extreme assaults on their senses. Momentary ecstasy gives way to prolonged ennui."

Buber's perceptive appreciation of the world is sacramental and mystical. This way of looking at the world involves no extraordinary type of religious experience related to special times and places. It is, rather, the redemption of everydayness by deliberation and insight. Buber puts it this way: "One should, and one must, truly live with all, but one should live with all in holiness, one should hallow all that one does in one's natural life. One eats in holiness, tastes the taste of food in holiness, and the table becomes an altar. One works in holiness; and he raises up the sparks that hide themselves in all tools. One walks in holiness across the fields, and the soft songs of all herbs, which they voice to God, enter into the song of our soul. One drinks in holiness to each other with one's companions, and it is as if they read together in the Torah. One dances the roundelay in holiness, and a brightness shines over the gathering. A husband is united with his wife in holiness, and the *shekina* rests over them."

This ode of Buber's is not a call to sane and sensible moderation but to fervor. How do you find this fervor? How do you experience this vivacity? By being fully present in the present moment. By paying complete attention to the person you are with or the task you are performing. By seeing the seen with all the strength of your life, hearing the heard with all the strength of your life, tasting the tasted with all the strength of your life.

Nikos Kazantzakis' famous Zorba the Greek is both Zorbatic and Buberian: "I've stopped thinking all the time," said Zorba, "of what happened yesterday. And stopped asking myself what's going to happen tomorrow. What's happening today, this minute, that's what I care about. I say, 'What are you doing at this moment, Zorba?' 'I'm kissing a woman.' 'Well, kiss her well, Zorba, and forget all the rest while you're doing it. There's nothing else on earth, just you and her.'"

As Roy Larson says, masochistic asceticism produces rusted-out work wrecks. A prissy libertinism produces pooped-out playboys and playmates. But mystical sacramentality produces truly sensuous men and women who, like the legendary cedars of Lebanon, are "full of sap and green" at every stage along life's way.

Sin makes consistently genuine, holy sensuousness difficult—not so much because the body or the lower self is unruly and in rebellion against the innocent mind; but because the mind is twisted. In sin, human beings voluntarily use their higher potentialities to create false ways of living in which the higher potentialities are denied. Once we free the comparatively innocent body from the totalitarian regimen of a sick and selfish mentality, then as redeemed body-persons we will begin to live. And to live is to love. Attaining this freedom is worth all the trouble: all the work and all the exercises that constitute an enlightened, organic asceticism of achieved spontaneity. This includes everything we do that is done thoughtfully and carefully: the way we chop wood and fetch water from the well, the way we tend animals and the flowers, the way we keep our house and prepare the food, the way we walk and run and play, the way we meet people and drive our cars. If all this work and play were done really well—as naturally, spontaneously, and creatively as possible—we would not need yoga or Zen or TM or est or any other device or technique, ancient or modern. Our creative work and our playful leisure would be the best possible preparation for prayer: for deep, de-egotizing encounters with one another, and holy communion with God. This is characteristic of Western Christian spirituality.

But we have come close to losing this secret of our tradition. How distressing, for instance, for me, in my retreat work, to visit seminaries, convents and monasteries that are situated in most ideal circumstances: in the country, with lawns, gardens and orchards, with none of the residents doing any of the outdoor work. Great amounts of money are expended hiring men to work, while the students, monks and nuns deprive themselves of such singular pleasure and privilege and the best possible preparation for both prayer and the apostolate. This is also true of many parish rectories. It seems to me that gardening and animal husbandry are as important as any academic aspect of education. No wonder we have so many spoiled priests and nuns, as well as uneducated but highly schooled masses of pseudosophisticated human beings.

What in youth is bound to be necessary discipline becomes in maturity a happy, holy act of reverence. In one instance, for example, and in this respect alone, I no longer clean my toilet to be virtuous. I do it because the toilet itself deserves it and I love it. I do not slam the door of my solitary hermitage for two reasons: one, for the sake of the birds and squirrels who, I imagine, are sensitive to noise; two, for the sake of the door itself.

If I may be permitted one more personal note. I just interrupted this writing and went for a swim. It is April 19. There is still snow on the ground at Nova Nada. These are our first spring days. The water is freezing. Then why swim? I've been enjoying all the shallow, surface qualities of the lake—watching the sun rise and set on it, canoeing on it. But I longed to plunge into its depths, participate in it more fully; there was just one thing to do: strip, dive in and swim. A positive not a punitive asceticism is involved. There is no way to come up with the exquisite delight then experienced (tingling and vibrating all over) except by going down into the cold, wet deeps of that glorious lake. We very often miss the big pleasures because we won't suffer some slight incommensurable preliminary pain. The point is that all discipline, all asceticism should lead to freedom—the freedom to live more fully and to love more passionately.

Freedom

There is nothing more desirable to every one of us than freedom; and yet very few of us ever manage to enjoy it on this earth. I have met two or three free men and women in my lifetime; that is all. Very few human beings today are even capable of freedom. Those who are able to be free are afraid. We are a frightened race—afraid of life, of death, of love, of ourselves, of other persons, of God, of failure, of sin, of risk, of public opinion, of criticism, of responsibility, of solitude and silence, of naked reality. We are driven by our fears into the slavery of a million momentary securities that level and freeze us into respectable robots and nicely behaved zombies.

Responsibility is the first characteristic of a free man. That means, literally and truly, the ability to respond. How many of us can respond truly and purely and spontaneously to the simple call of reality? To be able to respond means first of all being open, which seems to be nearly impossible for the average human being. Most of us close our minds and hearts. Even the few open people narrow down their perspective and fail to achieve a broadminded universality of love. Who wants to be vulnerable? Yet vulnerability is the price of openness.

The endless scope of a broad mind is the affirmation of everything. But how will we ever manage to squeeze all the usefulness out of the thing at hand, so readily manipulatable, if we have to stand back in reverent love and awe, wonderfully affirming and celebrating the intrinsic goodness of all being? The irresponsible busybody may have life; but he has no spirit. And without spirit he cannot transfigure matter. He can possess matter, pile it up, organize it, make it useful or waste it. But he cannot transfigure it. And the transfiguration of matter by spirit is the very stuff of life.

To be responsible means to see things as they really are. Such vision is made impossible by the masks we wear, the miseducation we get and transmit, the illusions we cultivate, the advertising we fall for, the social pressures we succumb to, the suprarational powers of the mind we let rot, the frantic pace we keep up, the ruts we lie down in. Only the free man, unattached to anything but in touch with the whole world, belonging to no one but in communion with everyone, is capable of seeing others as they really are. Only out of such freedom can a man love not some glorified image of himself but the really other and, above all, the Wholly Other.

Spontaneity and universal kinship are the hallmarks of a free man, and therefore, as rare as the free man. How many people, other than children, are at all capable of an unselfconscious spontaneous response? How many are even capable of wonder, the basis of all philosophy, theology and prayer? How many of us are free enough to declare our love openly and honestly, with no shameful connotations, to the old man next door, the schoolgirl who chats with us on the corner, the waitress who has served us well, the child who makes us laugh with joy, the co-worker or employer who has been so tolerant?

I know a man, a Mr. Blue type, who said "I love you" to a prostitute whose freely offered services he would not accept because he meant what he said: I love you. Healed and inspired by this love, the woman stopped her prostitution. My friend reminds me of the girl in that exquisitely beautiful movie *Rapture*, who loved a scarecrow into existence. She was so free to love that her neighbors thought she was crazy.

One of the reasons so many priests and nuns feel compelled to leave the priesthood and convent today is the lamentable fact that they were never taught—indeed, never allowed—to love humanly and freely. They were made to believe that deep, strong, personal love has no place in the celibate priesthood or religious life. Eventually they experience human love—and if it's human, it's also sexual, but not genital. They foolishly regard it as something diametrically opposed to celibacy and are driven by it into marriage.

Not only poorly trained priests and sisters have forfeited their freedom to love. Many people are so afraid or overwhelmed by the passion of love that at the first hint of it they institutionalize it, that is, they plunge it and themselves into the control system of marriage. It is strange and ironic how very often the love and freedom peter out in marriage. As the married couple resort more and more to the marital rights of possession ("You belong to me") and authority ("You may not rightly refuse me"), unexercised love dies. They have a married life all right, but no spirit of love.

I have yet to meet a person free enough for universal kinship. Everyone gets hung up on certain kinds, classes and types of people. But the great killer of universal love is an awesome trio: time, space and numbers. Countless love-relationships have been shipwrecked on these impervious elements. Very few friendships endure over a long period of time. People fall in and out of love with dozens of people with very little tenacity, perseverance and growth in depth. I suppose this is because there are so few deep relationships to begin with. At any rate, they don't withstand the test of time. Ceasing to love, refusing to care, is the worst kind of death. And the killing of friendship—by either positive or negative action—is the worst kind of murder. The inability to keep love alive is the most culpable human crime.

Our relationships survive the test of space no better than time. "Absence makes the heart grow fonder" is only true in rare cases or when the absence is of brief duration. Prolonged physical absence does kill love. This is sad and unfortunate, makes man a puny creature, and limits him absurdly.

The grossest, most common, and inexcusable of all human limitations is concerned with numbers. Here is the colossal fallacy: You can only be in love with one person. A woman falls in love with a man, stifles all her other loves, marries the man—and dies. Or a man says to a woman: "I love you." And she says: "Good; now you belong to me; do not love anyone else. Marry me. Then everyone will know you belong to me and no one else will love you."

This is the organized and socially acceptable form of love in our society. Almost no one is strong enough to break through this unnatural limitation. Almost no one is free to love more than one human being with passionate intensity. And is there anyone in our society free enough to tolerate the freedom of the great lover? The love I am proposing is no threat to spousal love. It is in fact, nothing like spousal love. Rather, a healthy and holy contractual permanent love between deeply wedded lovers overflows into glorious friendships.

I have been thinking about the freedom of man in general, and I am sufficiently distressed over our chained and fettered race. But when I reflect on the Christian and his paltry measure of freedom, I am appalled, because this is what Christianity is all about. Christ won freedom for himself and for us. It is the work of the Church to continue his freeing labor of love. God freed us from everything except himself. Christ delivered us from the law. The Gospel is the good news of our freedom. This truth is the great scandal of Christianity. It is the stone that is constantly being rejected by the builders.

We don't have the courage to face the awful freedom which contains in itself the crucial challenge of the Christian faith, the distinctive center that differentiates Christianity from every other religion. In other religions man tries to sanctify himself by rituals, regulations, and religious techniques. But Christianity frees us from rules and systems and relates by loving faith to the Risen Christ. The moment our religion becomes slavery to the law, we cease to be Christian.

There isn't a modern theologian who has written anything as hot to handle as St. Paul's doctrine on freedom: "No one is free to pass judgment on you in terms of what you eat, or drink or what you do on yearly or monthly feasts, or on the sabbath. All of these were but a shadow of things to come; the reality is in the Body of Christ.... If, then, you are dead with Christ from the elements of this world, why do you yet decree as though living in this world?... You are severed from Christ, you who would be justified by the law; you have fallen away from grace.... In Christ Jesus neither circumcision nor the lack of it counts for anything; only faith, which expresses itself through love" (Col. 2: 16-17, 20; Gal. 5:4, 6).

The law is a good crutch. But the Christian must learn to transcend the law. Christian love demands that we grow up into the full stature of Christ, become free with the freedom of the children of God and throw away the crutches. The man who can walk on water in faith does not wear a bathing suit just in case. The man who lives by love does not lean on the law just in case. How urgently we need to know today that all but free men get swallowed up in the system! Freedom in the Church is the only way out of the institutional bind.

Notes

[1] Louis Monden, S. J., *Sin, Liberty and Law*, (New York: Sheed and Ward, 1965), pp. 122–23.

[2] Josef Pieper, *In Tune with the World*, translated by Richard and Clara Winston (Chicago: Franciscan Herald Press, 1973), p. 19.

[3] *Ibid.*, p. 53.

[4] Davis, *Body as Spirit*, p. 34.

[5] John Wren-Lewis, *What Shall We Tell the Children?* (London: Constable, 1971), p. 152.

Chapter 6
Our Daily Bread

"Man is what he eats." Although Ludwig Feuerbach, a German materialistic philosopher of the nineteenth century, did not know it at the time, in that statement he was expressing the most religious idea of man. But Scripture said it long before Feuerbach.

What is man's primeval experience? In the Bible's sensuous story of creation, man is presented as a being hungry for God. His life depends on the whole world as a sacrament of communion with God. The original fall of man is his non-Eucharistic life in a non-Eucharistic world. The fall is not that man preferred the world to God, distorted the balance between spiritual and material, but that he made the world *material.* whereas he was to have transformed it into "life in God," filled with meaning and spirit.

God created the world transparent and Eucharistic. By sensuously feasting on that world, man was meant to drink in God. In Genesis, God instructs man to eat of the earth. Man must eat in order to live; he must take the world into his body and transform it into himself, into flesh and blood. He is indeed that which he eats, and the whole world is presented as one all-embracing banquet table for him. This image of the banquet remains the central image of life throughout the whole Bible. It is the image of life at its creation and also the image of life at its end and fulfillment: . . . "That you eat and drink at my table, in my Kingdom," (Luke 22:30). This kind of sensuousness runs right through the Scriptures, shaping the origins of the Judeo-Christian tradition, reaching a glorious climax in the New Testament, especially in Christ himself.

Bread and Wine

Religious experience is unfortunately thickly overlaid by theological speculation. The reality of God becomes increasingly submerged beneath theories that fruitlessly attempt to forge a connection between the personal, glorified, ascended Christ of faith and the lifeless, impersonal objects of bread and wine. This is not only a useless endeavor; it is also a very damaging procedure.

We are now in a vicious circle where we are forced to rediscover through an argument, or a whole series of arguments, what was originally lost through an argument or a whole series of arguments. It's like suddenly finding yourself in the middle of a woods, the most beautiful place you've ever seen. You can't stay there, and you have a very difficult time finding your way out. But you make a pathway, even though it is very circuitous and wide of the mark. Subsequently lots of people hear about your experience of that beautiful spot and they all take your lost route to get there. No one ends up there directly and immediately the way you did the first time.

That is the kind of theological predicament we are in today because we are excessively committed to speculation and reflection. Though they are an integral part of experience, they can veil and obfuscate as well as reveal and clarify. With centuries of speculation we may never get back to the original experience—an experience that the speculative reflections were meant to preserve and present to us. It is a strange situation: the doctrine about an experience has become more real than the experience.

Most of the theological discussions about the presence of God in Eucharistic bread and wine have become insignificant if not bizarre because we've lost sight of the whole picture and lost track of the connections. The three synoptic evangelists make it very clear that the whole Gospel narration concerns itself with one single message. That one message permeates all the events of our Lord's life: God's presence in all things, and in a focused, concentrated way: his presence in the bread. We pack bread and wine full of meaning and then allow these simple basic elements of human existence to carry us away into supernatural realms of life and love.

When Jesus said, "This is my Body," he was not simply referring to an ordinary, inorganic, lifeless object called bread, that got miraculously changed into his Body. The bread was as sacred as ever and so was the wine. What was significant—highly and newly significant—was the "Last Supper," the "Passover meal." Outside of that context the same thing would not have happened. If Jesus had said the same thing at another time in the bakeries of Jerusalem, nothing like the transubstantiation at the Last Supper would have occurred. What he did at the Passover meal was not a bit of magic or shamanism. It was the festive fulfillment of all that went before in the history of the Jews and was now being brought to fruition in Christ. What happened in the Cenacle was a crucial, transitional event. It wasn't arbitrary. God was already there, present in the bread. The revolutionary aspect of it was Christ's saying: "This is my body" and "This is my Blood."

On the eve of many a revolutionary event—the Irish Rebellion, the defense of the Alamo, the Crucifixion of Good Friday—real life as well as literature presents the participants meeting in an attic, gathering round a table, sharing bread and drink. Scripture tells us that Christ desired with passionate intensity to eat the Passover meal with his disciples before he suffered (Luke 22:15).

The evangelists seem fascinated by the presence of Judas at

the Last Supper and rightly so. His behavior relates significantly to the meaning of the Eucharist. The Psalmist says, "Even my friend who had my trust and partook of my bread has raised his heel against me" (Ps. 41:10). According to John 13:30, "no sooner had Judas eaten the morsel than he went out." His absence from the communion of his brethren, from the table fellowship, was not only an act of disloyalty but a sacrilege— because of the inherent holiness of bread.

This is why attendance at Sunday Mass, the Eucharistic banquet, is a matter of ultimate seriousness. We are involved in far more than weekly fellowship. We gather with our brothers to celebrate the fact that bread is holy. Therefore every created thing is holy and we are at home in creation and in love with God.

Our Western mentality is so prosaic and secular that the Eucharistic mystery of life tends to escape us. A European missionary in Africa wanted to impress on his people the clear distinction between a consecrated and an unconsecrated host. He held up an unconsecrated one and said, "What is this?" In unison the Africans said, "the Body of Christ." The European missionary said, "You are absolutely wrong!" In order to demonstrate, he crumbled the host in his hand, threw it on the floor, and trampled on it.

The Africans were shocked, not because they continued to believe that the host was consecrated, and therefore the Body and Blood of Christ, but because it was sacred in itself, inherently, overwhelmingly sacred as bread. It was the fruit of the earth, of the relentless sun, of the deluge of water flooding the fields. It was the fruit of God's benevolence and of his irrepressible fury, and therefore already sacred, already God, already mysteriously ready to be the Body and Blood of Christ. They regarded everything as a direct manifestation of the ubiquitous presence of God. So they were more in tune with reality than was the European missionary who isolated the Eucharist and made it an artificial sort of device, a bit of spooky religion rather than the culmination of the ongoing growth of the spirit in the world. We misconstrue the meaning and misuse the sacrament itself when by religious pronouncements of faith we try to switch the profane into the sacred and wrest God from above. Food is already holy, not profane, and may never under any circumstances be desecrated, even as a possible demonstration of something that could be more sacred. We say grace before our meals—not to make our food holy, but to acknowledge gratefully that it is already holy. We don't gobble our food, play with it, or throw it around, because food is too sacred to be violated. A "food war" I witnessed in a college cafeteria was one of the most painful desecrations of sacred matter that I have ever suffered.

Religious ceremonies don't create holiness. What they do is usher us into the holiness of God, the holiness that was already there permeating the universe. Sacraments are tools of denuminization, making available and bearable the dazzling dimension of the Numinous, the Holy Other, while they, at the same time, protect the sacramental participants from heaven and hell. Heaven and hell aren't separate cloistered places apart from the world. They are the angelic and demoniac dimensions of this world. What the sacrament does is cushion and soften the relentless passion of God breaking through. Otherwise we would be shattered. "It is a fearful thing to fall into the hands of the living God" (Heb. 10:31). The sacraments prevent us from being devoured by the fierce and fiery love of God. Notice how the momentum of the Mass moves along, reaches a peak, and comes to an end. Notice how Christ comes, lingers for a while, very briefly in communion, and then disappears. Once again: shades of the heroic cowboy!

Jesus did not institute a sacrament of the Eucharist. He entered into the sacramentality of the universe, making effective already existing sacraments by his suffering and death, his descent into Sheol, into the jaws of hell, the terrible awful mouth of God.

Earth has more than one realm. It has a depth that is the greedy mouth of God. Into that awful abyss our most daring men, our prophets, have bellowed their words. But this abyss does not give of its treasure very readily or very easily. Not that it does not deliver its deep profound secret, its ultimate treasure. It does. But not until the Son of God clothed in the clouds, comes forth from the bridal chamber and stands in stunning, stirring mystery as the bewildering and bewitching stranger, the Beyond in our midst. That is the meaning of the Eucharist. We await our host, only to find that "he comes crashing up through the floor and riding into the heights. He burns a hole in the room by coming suddenly, not gradually. He does not come in flat-footedness, but in holy awe. He is not from among the guests. He is the Miraculous Rider on his way from the abyss to the heights and back again."[1]

"Not by Bread Alone"

In the desert Christ is tempted to turn stones into bread. He refuses, and tells the devil, "Man shall not live by bread alone" (Matt. 4:4). In other words, man does not live only on bread-food but by every kind of food—including stones (a symbol of death).

Man does not live on bread alone "but by every word that proceeds from the mouth of God" (Matt. 4:4). Eating and drinking the Word of God is a concept found throughout the entire Bible. We feed on the Word of God not only through the bread and wine of the Eucharist, but through Sacred Scripture and other spiritual reading.

Most of us take pains to avoid the consequences of an unfed and unexercised body. We are less concerned over our unfed and unexercised minds. Like the body, the mind must be nourished. Reading is essential. Bodies feed on bodies. Minds feed on minds. You may have spread out before you the best selection of food in the world. None of it will do your body any good unless you select some of it and put it into your stomach. You may also be surrounded by the best minds in the world by having at your disposal their literary productions. None of this will do you any good unless you select some of it and put it into your own mind.

There you have a definition of reading—a way of feeding your mind upon a mind richer than your own. When you read a man's book you grow rich with the richness of his mind. In the assimilation of his ideas your own mind is exercised and grows muscular and healthy.

But this is true only of real reading—a muscular activity of the whole mind. Not just the abstract intellect speculating, conceptualizing—working its way inexorably into truth by sharp analysis and steadfast logic; but the suprarational powers of the mind, too, the intuitive and contemplative forces wooing and charming their way into truth, or better, inviting truth to come to them by the invincible attraction and receptivity of love.

We must not read to pass the time away. What an unforgivable waste of time and intelligence! Nor must we read to escape from reality, particularly the reality of ourselves and the boredom of our own company. This kind of reading does nothing for the mind. Nothing happens in the mind; the time simply passes and we lose forever an opportunity to be better than we are.

Reading is a sure test of the mind's well-being. The body that has no appetite for food is sick. So is the mind that does not hunger for more truth, a deeper understanding, a wider perspective, a brighter vision. This is the criterion of human vitality. Deny the body food long enough and you will have a corpse. Nothing very attractive about a corpse. Starve the mind long enough and you have something even more repulsive, a spiritual corpse; mindlessness, or, if you will, a trousered ape.

To go for months without reading a decent thoughtful book is to class ourselves unmistakably with the mindless majority. Let me repeat: a good reading habit—not a university—is the only sure test of the mind's well-being.

But it has got to be more than casual reading. One cannot acquire a classical shape of mind or even, for that matter, a decent human mind, in odd half hours found by chance in the indeliberate course of a day or a week. Reading must be pursued with seriousness and regularity in a disciplined daily program. It must take precedence over most things, such as golf, bridge, television, ordinary conversation.

Most men beg off on account of fatigue. I am as fatigued as the next fellow, perhaps more so most of the time. I know the problem by experience. There are more ways to be recreated than by sleep. The answer to fatigue is vitality which is won, primarily, by food and exercise, secondarily, by relaxation. Relaxation alone merely produces flabbiness of mind which brings on fatigue sooner and surer.

The problem of time remains. We must face it. That is why I must emphasize the importance of selection. We cannot eat everything; we must select what is best for the body. We cannot read everything; we must select what is best for the mind. We must read discriminately.

The first kind of discrimination we must bring to bear in our choice of reading matter is negative. We act the way we think. We think about the things that have entered into our minds through our eyes and ears. Ralph Waldo Emerson said, a man is what he thinks of most of the day. If our minds are full of foolishness we act foolishly. If our minds are full of petty, unimportant things we are bound to become shallow. It is murder to fill the stomach with garbage. It is spiritual suicide to fill the mind with junk. The negative principle keeps out of the mind whatever is unworthy of it, whatever could not possibly enrich it.

The second kind of discrimination is positive. Since time and energy are so scarce they must be conserved with extreme care. There is not ever enough time and energy to read what is good. We can only afford to read what is best. There must be a strict order of selectivity. We must begin with what is indispensable, with the books we cannot get along without. The just man lives by faith. Faith is man's response to God's revelation of himself. If a man is going to live by faith then he must drink long and deep from the fountains of revelation: Scripture and tradition. It is the duty of theologians to explore and reexamine the sources of revelation and to express the Divine Word in clear and meaningful language, so that all men today and tomorrow and tomorrow and tomorrow may be sustained by the word of God, so that they may not only know their faith, but through their faith, full of insight and understanding, may know God by experience, by a personal loving encounter. As Frank Sheed says, a man who does not feed his mind on theology is living in the suburbs of reality, not in reality. And so we see why spiritual reading is indispensable.

Without spiritual reading—unless one finds some substitute—there is no possibility of advancing in the spiritual life, or even persevering in it. Spiritual reading provides a compensation for the rapid de-Christianizing of our present-day environment. Just as workmen who cannot get out to the ballpark turn directly to the sports pages to keep in touch, so the Christian in an indifferent atmosphere turns to spiritual reading to keep him in vital contact with the most real world—spiritual reality. Otherwise, as the saying goes, "out of sight, out of mind."

Another purpose of spiritual reading is to "trap" us into praying. It serves as a hallway into meditation where the introductions and amenities are taken care of before entering into more personal conversation with God. Even the great Teresa of Avila admitted she could not meditate for years without the help of a book.

No doubt at the outset this type of reading may seem as taste-less as the manna did to the Israelites on the long desert trek from Egypt. For us as well the taste of "onions" will still be strong and it will take some time to become accustomed to this new food. But with a little patience and determination, we shall ac-quire the habit, the taste for spiritual food—then we shall "taste and see how good the Lord is" (Ps. 34:9).

Even with spiritual reading we must be fussy. There is an order of importance. Christ is God's most perfect and complete revelation of himself. Christ is God in his most attractive form. We must first of all steep and saturate the mind with Christ; not once but all the time. The Gospels, therefore, should hold the first and last place in our spiritual reading. They make up the vertical backbone, all else is horizontal vertebrae. The New Testament wears better than any other book, inexhaustibly rich with veins that never play out. In the latter period of her life, a time of extreme dryness and suffering, St. Thérèse of Lisieux said that all other books gave her a sort of malaise except the Gospels, a copy of which she wore over her heart. A contem-porary Frenchman, Charles de Foucauld, the Apostle of the Sahara, prescribes the reading of the Gospels as a direct route to contemplation.

We must try not to read the inspired account of our Lord's life and words as past history but as presently happening before our eyes. The words of Christ are always in the present tense; on his own testimony, they "shall not pass away" (Luke 21:33). To make the Gospels come alive in our own modern milieu, the commentaries and popular lives of Christ are invaluable.

Next in importance are the great classics. A classic is a book that is contemporaneous with every age. It is that great, that basic, and that peculiarly and perseveringly pertinent to man, that is significant to all men everywhere, at any time. I am think-ing of the works of Augustine, Thomas Aquinas, Bonaventure, Francis de Sales, John of the Cross, Teresa of Avila, Elizabeth of the Trinity, *The Little Flowers of St. Francis,* the *Autobiography of St. Thérèse of Lisieux,* and more. Another kind of book that belongs in the primary class is the kind that gives an integral, well-balanced, comprehensive perspective of the whole life of the spirit, the total Christian life. Frank Sheed's books do this well on the didactic or expository level, as does Abraham Heschel's *Between God and Man.* The *Chronicles of Narnia* are incomparable on the mythical level, as are other works by C.S. Lewis. Paul VI's encyclical *Ecclesiam Suam* (1964) is an outstanding summation of the masters of the spiritual life, and John XXIII's *Pacem in Terris* (1963) is one of the most pertinent documents of our age.

Besides the objective criterion of what to read there is a subjective norm: one ought to read in his vein; which means that one ought to explore and experiment until he discovers what is best for him, most pertinent and timely. The neighbor's happy discovery may be poison for you. (There is a central vein that runs through humanity, though; and that is why you have best sellers.)

Besides knowing that one should read and what one should read, it is important to know how to read. Let me urge you to try Mortimer Adler's *How To Read a Book* and Ernest Dimnet's *The Art of Thinking.* Both of these are classics on the subject of reading. Studying them is an education in itself.

In the Middle Ages, men put their whole bodies, as well as their whole minds into spiritual reading; it was literally a physical as well as spiritual exercise. They read, not as today, principally with the eyes, but with the lips and ears as well. Spiritual reading was rightly regarded as an "exercise," that is, something done not merely for pleasure but with an eye to perfecting a skill or virtue. In this sense St. Ignatius calls his famous formula for retreats *The Spiritual Exercises.* In our days of silent reading, we can compensate by reading slowly, ruminating like cattle cropping grass. If at the beginning we read from curiosity, it is not a dead-end curiosity but a healthy one that goes on to love, just as Zacchaeus' climb up into a sycamore tree was the prelude to having Christ as his supper guest. (Cf. Luke 19:2-6.)

We do not read to fill our minds with facts. As Frank Sheed puts it so well, "Facts can be pushed into the mind like books into a bag; and as usefully. Tuck in as many books as you please and the bag has still gained nothing. All that happens is that it bulges." We read for wisdom, which is knowledge become our very own, assimilated into our bloodstream by a real, not rational, assent of the whole mind—intellect and will. This is what the ancients meant by the phrase "learning by heart."

Biblical Humor

If some of us find Scripture tasteless reading, perhaps we do not understand its style. Revelation language is very similar to the puns and witticisms in our everyday speech. They both depend on ambiguity to obtain their effects.

A pun is a sign that is simultaneously and successfully taken as a constitutive part of two or more symbols. The genius of puns in the context of religion is that they can carry us into the heart of religious truth and give us fleeting glimpses of who God is and who we can be while we are still deeply committed to workaday affairs and worldly concepts.

Witticisms are locutions, or more properly the wrecks of locutions, which must be taken in two or more logically or psychologically incompatible senses at once. They derail rational discourse and upset the status quo of a stale mind at the point where they occur. Lively persons who make witty and wise breakthroughs become witnesses of the Living God. They break through conventional pious routine and he who "alone is holy" shines through their transparent personalities. They break through formulas and propositions and stand still before the incalculable and unspeakably wonderful mystery of God. Wit leads us to the void; in wit we encounter non-being, a central human but difficult concept. Puns enrich values and meanings. Wit, like the parables of Jesus or Zen koans, explodes them. Wit shocks us out of our mental ruts the way the problem of evil jolts us out of religious apathy. The only religious solution to the problem of evil is conversion —metanoia—an upset and revision of our religious understanding and of our apprehension of self. After experiencing disaster on a certain theological and conceptual level and the simultaneous or subsequent awakening of our mythopoeic and existential awareness, we may never be quite the same again. With the painful experience of wit we ordinarily turn from religion as problem-solving to religious worship and to adoration, the purest kind of prayer.

The Bible itself, far from a series of straight assertions, is a wonderful collection of puns and witticisms and ought to be read accordingly. We often misunderstand it by an interpretation that is too solemn and sober. The Bible scores its points not in the direct, blunt, crashing style of a bowling alley champ, but in the way a pool shark does, by careening each shot off several cushions, from different sides. We gain a better understanding of the Bible not by henpecking it, but by absorbing and assimilating the cumulative meaning of the deluge of ambiguous puns and witticisms and seductive nuances by which we have been inundated.

As Chesterton so wisely put it, you can have all the solemnity you want in your neckties, but when it comes to something as important as sex, death, or religion, you must have mirth or you will have madness. It makes sense that the sexiest man who ever lived, the world's central religious figure who overcame death, should be the big surprise, the final incongruity, the complete humorist, Jesus Christ. He was born with the gift of laughter and a sense that the world was mad.

By his life and teaching, Jesus revealed that all news is good news. Once you grasp the mighty significance of that you shed all forms of neurotic anxiety and become as playful as a child, as witty as a clown, and holy with the holiness of God. Only a man of deep faith can live humorously and merrily, as did Thomas More, who "served God wittily in the tangle of his mind." The opposite of joy is not sorrow but unbelief.

The Gospels are full of humor. I suspect there is a lot more humor there than even the evangelists knew about. After all, they were so overwhelmed by the power and majesty of Christ and his supremely serious mission that they were apt to miss his levity and jollity. There is certainly plenty of humor that the scriptural exegetes don't seem to recognize. They torture literal significance from phrases first coined to blast a literal interest.

Many important passages and crucial insights of the Gospel cannot be rightly understood unless interpreted humorously. Consider, for instance, the famous story of the unjust steward in Luke 16:1-9. This is a joke so preposterous that it has got to mean the opposite of what is being said. And if Christ used sober prose when he said it is "easier for the heavens and the earth to pass away than for a single stroke of the letter of the law to fall" (Luke 16:17), then he spoke falsely.

At times Jesus is teasing and taunting the apostles and what he says so mockingly can only be understood in that lighthearted sense. At other times, in the face of pomposity and pharisaical materialism, he is so outraged, as in Matthew 5:27-28, that he simply laughs away all righteous pretense. There are magnificent examples of hyperbole in the Gospels, but if taken too seriously and literally (Matt. 7:1, for instance), followers of Christ would be utterly dehumanized. Can you imagine the shape of the Church or of the State or even a monastery if we did not judge! How do we account for the Lord's preference for sinners and the delightful way he twiddled the truth out of simple saucy women? His jaunty repartee with the woman at the well and the Canaanite woman is full of fun and pleasure.

Christ spoke the truth in poetry, scintillating epigrams, and pithy puns—the sort of stuff you would remember even if, at the moment, you did not understand. That is why the New Testament is such a classic and the greatest meditation book in the world. We need more than mental acuity to fathom it. We need to be wholly immersed in the mystery of the ineffable God who from all eternity speaks one word—a word which reaches its perfection and fullness in Christ so that nothing remains to be said.

The idea behind all sacred writing is to convey a deeper meaning than the literal words contain, the truth of which must be seen by man internally. To understand literally is one thing, to understand psychologically is another. "Thou shalt not murder in thy heart" is the psychological meaning of "Thou shalt not kill." The literal commandment is "Thou shalt not commit adultery." But its deeper, psychological meaning has to do with mixing different doctrines and different teachings, whoring after other gods. The psychological meaning of "Thou shalt not steal" refers to a proud and foolish attitude by which we take everything for granted and ascribe everything to ourselves.

Christ transformed literal into psychological meaning, thus drawing his followers into a deeper level of understanding, into individual evolution and rebirth. Christ—as psychological meaning—is always crucified by those who can only take in literal, sense-based meaning.

Communication between the literal and psychological levels is extremely difficult. Christ came to bridge the gap, to *passover* from the shallow to the deep level. To passover—which is exactly what Christ did—is to attain the kingdom of heaven. He urges all of us to follow him into realized union with his Father in heaven. But direct contact with God is difficult. The evolution involved in this *passover* is a veritable revolution. The contact is established by prayer. Momentum is maintained by prayer.

A Cry of the Heart

In Luke's Gospel, after Christ taught his disciples the Our Father, he went on to speak of the necessity of persistence in prayer. According to his parables, prayer is not easily answered. One must pray with "shameless impudence." I think of the enterprising little boy who met me in a busy store in Halifax. He wanted a dime but didn't simply ask for it. Instead he offered to do two or three clever tumbles and suggested that if I liked them I might give him a dime. He was no ordinary little beggar. He did his tumbles and I gave him all the money I had. That kind of importunity must characterize our prayer. It is not because God, our Father, is reluctant to answer prayer; it is due to a difficulty inherent in the nature of things. God and man are not on the same level. The shallow level of which we tend to live is out of touch with the deeps. Many difficulties stand in the way. That is why Christ insists that we "ought always to pray and not to faint" (Luke 18:1).

Communication not only with the ground but the underground of our being, the divine level itself, is impeded by any trace of vanity, self-conceit or arrogance. That is why so much is said in the Gospels about the purification of the emotions. The greatest impurity in man comes from the feelings of self–righteousness, self-complacency, and superiority. This point is made most emphatically in the parable about the Pharisee and the publican who went into the temple to pray (Luke 18:9-14).

To pray—to get in touch with the underground of our being—a person must know and feel he is nothing, in comparison with the ineffable being that reaches up and touches him from what the mystics Meister Eckhart and Jakob Böhme called the *ungrund* and what I call the *underground*. Unless we feel that we are nothing, prayer is useless. We are pure in our emotional life to the extent that we feel our own nothingness, our own ignorance, and our own helplessness. This is what Christ is referring to (Matt. 6:5-6) when he speaks of praying out of our own inner truth, and not out of our vanity. That is why the Christian at prayer does not always sit in a serene and tranquil posture of stillness and receptivity. Sometimes he pounds his fists on the wall or paces the floor; sometimes, like Job, he argues with God (Job 10:1-3 *et al.*) or, like Jacob, wrestles with him and comes out maimed for life (Gen. 32:24-25); sometimes he is so overwhelmed by Divine Providence that he dances joyfully like David in his Lord's presence (2 Sam. 6:14). In general, whenever he enters into prayer he assumes he may not come out alive.

To "go into your room and shut the door" (Matt. 6:6) means to go right into the ground of your being, your deepest self, as opposed to your shallow ego that is nothing more than a servant of the public, an invented social myth, or a seeker of reward, success and outer promise. It is only the interior, stable, recollected man that can obtain response to prayer. The external, worldly side of man, the inflated ego full of pretensions, cannot pray.

To receive a response to prayer, prayer must be of a certain quality and fulfill certain conditions. It must spring from an absolutely pure feeling; otherwise it cannot reach its goal. The sign given by the Gospels to designate the *passover*—from the ego level to the ground of being—is love of neighbor, living in enlightened harmony with all that is, with special emphasis on human relationships. The Lord's Prayer is always answered. No other prayer is answered unless it is in accord with the Lord's Prayer.

Jesus does, indeed, say: "Ask and you shall receive" (John 16:24), but we've got to unpack the meaning of that word "ask." Through prayer we elicit a response from the deepest level of the universe, the God-level. Seen rightly, the universe is response to request. The scientist works confidently, believing he will get a response from the physical universe as a result of his experiments, theories and efforts, all of which comprise his request. This is a kind of prayer; he gets a response if he asks the right way. It requires time, trouble, effort, and, above all, faith. If the scientist, or for that matter, the baker and candlestick maker, do not get what they were looking for, it is not because the universe is at fault, but because the form of their request was wrong. The baker must learn how to bake better—that is, how to *ask* better. To ask is to request. We live in a very responsive universe, visible and invisible, so that both the scientist and the man of prayer who ask rightly can expect a response.

Everything depends upon the quality of prayer. If our prayer is casual, mechanized and repetitive, it gets us nowhere. We are stuck on the shallow level of the ego. We remain incomplete, unevolved. Prayer must be persisted in, but as Christ said: "When you pray, use not vain repetitions" (Matt. 6:7). The scientist looking for his response in the natural universe varies his request patiently and inventively until he comes up with the right one. The man of prayer must be in faithful and insightful rapport with the spiritual universe, learning by trial and error, and humble perseverance, how to ask.

With all the new emphases on prayer it must come as a surprise to people who notice that Jesus never taught prayer until his disciples begged him to teach them to pray. Then, of course, he did. But until then and forever after, all his energy was spent in seducing them into the mystery, enticing them to live. To him prayer was a cry of the heart. If he could get them to live—really live—they would pray. Prayers that do not match our deeds are a cheap waste of time. Prayers that do not come from the ground of our being and express our own inner truth are a caricature of prayer, a parody of someone else's experience of God.

Prayer must be passionate. It is the expression in word and gesture of our ultimate concern, of what we take most seriously. The personal and specific ways in which we suffer life provide the only valid foundation for prayer. Rooting prayer in the real precludes pious piffle. When Christ responded to his disciples' plea for a lesson in prayer, he simply summed up for them, in existential concreteness, the meaning of the Exodus, the passover from slavery to freedom, the personal desert experience of everyman. The Our Father is the "prayer of the heart" par excellence. Though hearty, it is untainted by any form of sentimentality. It is pure passion directed by the "long view" toward the "one thing" necessary. This may impress you more profoundly if you meditate on the Lord's Prayer backwards. For many years now I have personally found this to be a most rewarding meditative practice. It was a delightful surprise, therefore, to find it recommended by Orthodox Archbishop Bloom in a book called *Living Prayer* (1966).

Deliver us from evil. Existentially, that's got to be our first petition. We've got to recognize the human predicament, our stuck-in-the-mud condition, our inability to save ourselves, our need for a Redeemer. Ontological humility is the first step toward prayer. But what we need to be delivered from most of all are all the subtle forms of evil, the sins of the just. We need to worry much more about our minor virtues than our major vices, about our good ruts rather than our bad ruts.

Corruptio optimi pessima. The corruption of the best things is the worst corruption. That's what some of the stout ages of the past had to worry about. But it is not our modern vice. Few of us ever rise to the best, and consequently few of us descend to the depths. *Corruptio melioris pejor* seems more suited to us, and we could translate it: The corruption of what is ok produces what is pretty bad. The evil to which modern man is addicted is a respectable form of vulgarity. Being vulgar has nothing to do with being unschooled. The untutored man simply is who he is, and is thus incapable of vulgarity. Real-life situations draw him out, which is the literal meaning of education. Vulgarity occurs when people who happen to have some schooling assume that they are educated. This false assumption, with all its pomp and circumstance, leads to a hypocritical way of life that is grotesque and truly vulgar. Most of us perish honorably by falling from our ok condition to being pretty bad. Our uneducated or, at best, half-educated manner of existence is hardly noticeable since all of us have agreed to be less than ourselves. The power and image of God in us begins to fade as we cling to conventional values, to what is respectable, the right thing to do, the latest opinion, the most recent poll. Aiming at being ok, we end up being pretty bad. This, I am suggesting, is real vulgarity, an okness or mediocrity reflected in the plethora of pretty bad movies and books that reach the top, from Erich Segal to Erica Jong.

Religion has been vulgarized in similar ways. It tends to float in a vacuum until it somehow attaches itself to the kind of values that are in general fashion. When religion was an integral part of vocation and work and the life of a people closely bound together in their material aims, with common values that permeated the community, it emerged as the highest dimension of this social life. It might be individually good, poor or indifferent, but it was as real as the life was real. It was honest.

Divorced now by circumstances from common life and work, religion has become individualized, self-centered, introspective, and detached; becoming more and more prone to all the illusions of ritualism and pseudomysticism. Because the Church has tried for so long to be ok, it is now in pretty bad shape. If it seems to be alive and well, this may be due to questionable criteria.

Lead us not into temptation. This is not a plea to be spared all trials and tribulations. It is no attempt to prayerfully camouflage a reprehensible desire to retreat from life, to evade the moral battleground. It is a prayer for the conservation of moral energy. We have little time and a limited supply of energy. We cannot afford superfluous, superficial or irrelevant temptations. The crucial, inescapable ones are enough for anyone. We pray then to be tempted if we must, but not beyond the possibilities of our strength.

As Joachim Jeremias suggests, this petition would be more correctly rendered: "Let us not succumb to temptation."[2] What is requested is not preservation from temptation but preservation in temptation. This is corroborated by an ancient extracanonical saying which a long tradition believes Jesus spoke on that last evening, prior to the prayer in Gethsemani: "No man can obtain the kingdom of God that hath not passed through temptation."[3]

This is a humble prayer, a realistic one. We know how prone we are to choose sin, to choose what is nasty and evil instead of God. "Let anyone who thinks he stands [untempted at all] take heed lest he fall." (1 Cor. 10:12). We implore God not to put too great a strain on us: not to let us get into too difficult a situation.

Forgive us our trespasses as we forgive those who trespass against us. This is truly responsible prayer when we will not beg for forgiveness from God without promising forgiveness to those who have hurt us. It is an existential prayer because we put our lives on the line and make our deeds match our words. It is a liberating prayer because we not only get rid of external baggage and bondage but all that stuff on the inside of us that stifles the mind and clutters the heart.

"By this all men will know that you are my disciples, if you have love one for another" (John 13:35). This was our Lord's last exhortation to his disciples. He insists on mutual charity because when we put it into practice it brings all the rest in its train. St. Paul says, "He who loves his neighbor has fulfilled the law" (Rom. 13:8). Christ didn't come to give us a doctrine that would make us all happy materially. He said, "Seek first the Kingdom of God and his justice and all these things shall be added unto you" (Matt. 6:33)—all these things will fall into place. When our love of God is perfect we are perfect. That means we can live harmoniously with the universe. It means especially that we never offend unnecessarily another human being. We move out of Egypt, out of our deadness, and begin to follow Christ when we forgive everyone and forget everything except Christ and him crucified.

Give us this day our daily bread. According to Scripture scholars, the original version of this petition was "our bread for tomorrow give us today." The reference is to the bread of life, both heavenly and earthly. There seems to be a striking resemblance between contemporary youth and the early Christians. They seek the bread of life and are frustrated, often angered, when we feed them stones. They want the bread, the mystical life, today; are miffed and rightly so, when we try to enthrall them with the future. I am not talking about "instant" mysticism; and, in this case neither are they. What is being sought, with very little help from most Christian churches and schools, is appropriate measures of mystical life now. There is no reason why the average priest should not be able to lead the average student or parishioner into the prayer of quiet within a reasonably short time.

The prayer for daily bread is expressed hunger for God, for his self-disclosures, his divine touches, his sustaining presence. By the same token it is a plea, involving efficacious desire, for enlightened openness and receptivity, the watchfulness and insight necessary to discern and enjoy the tremendous and fascinating everywhereness of God. *Eros* and *Agape* converge as man is lifted up by the partially fulfilled promise of things into ever higher and holier pursuits, until he is devoured by the consuming fire of God's love.

Thy will be done. In any other context this would be a proclamation that would make me suspicious, if not outrightly disbelieving. It is bandied about so blithely by pious people that it now seems to be our most popular religious cliché. The total commitment, final surrender, and wild abandonment required to say this brief prayer with any degree of authenticity makes it an almost impossible achievement. What turns the tide and prepares man for the most perilous pinnacle of all human ventures is the passionate prayer that precedes it, a prayer that is matched by heroic deeds. No one but saints and madmen make this petition honestly.

Thy Kingdom come. Here is the prayer of the God-centered man, willing to be spent, lost, forgotten, ignored, persecuted—anything for the Kingdom of God. "The Kingdom of God is at hand" (Mark 1:15). Christ started it. We must finish it by the work of our hands, a labor of love. *Homo faber:* man is a maker, an artist, a creator. But nothing he does makes such sense unless it has something to do with building the Kingdom. What does Christ mean by the Kingdom? He means the fullness of being human, the experience of personal passionate presence. Labor leads to leisure, a holy leisure full of action so pure, refined, recollected and festive that it needs no reason or purpose outside of itself for its justification.

This highest kind of action is called contemplation and is what occupies creative man at the heart of the Kingdom. Such a wise man is wholly immersed in existential Christian living, in "eschatology becoming actualized." In other words, the meaning of existence consists in this: just as God through the Passion of Christ continues to become man, so man continues to become God.

Hallowed be thy name. No preoccupation with our plans, projects, programs. No tooting my own horn or bellowing my own name. And no mouthing of his: neither in fervor nor in vain. It is hard to say who is more guilty of sin; the holy name-dropping priest or the blasphemer. But this we know: the silent, awed man, lost in adoration of God, hallows his sacred name.

Thou who art in heaven. Almost ready for the perfect prayer, the real prayer of the Spirit, toward which every inspired word of the Lord's Prayer and every deed of our daily lives—sacred and profane—has been leading us, we hesitate momentarily, catch our breath, and review our human condition: our finite, fragile nature and the infinite transcendence of Him who Is. But bridging the gap we behold the Man who in the power of the Spirit reconciles opposites and dissolves polarities, as he gathers the multiplicity of beings into the One, brings to complete fruition the yearning and yielding of all creatures by a perfect, deathless act of love, and unites forever, at least at the bedrock of being, God and man.

This is the experience of filiation. We now know what it means to be sons of God. The Spirit is released in us. As St. Paul said, "we do not know how to pray" (Rom. 8:26). But when we let the Spirit break through, overcoming our ignorance and inadequacy, conforming us to Christ, a cry is heard over all the earth. It is the mighty, mysterious prayer of the Spirit, a cry of the heart, of the Sacred Heart. It is the Spirit crying "Abba" in us: *Our Father.*

Notes

[1]C.D. Keyes, *God or Ichabod? A Non-Violent Christian Nihilism* (Cincinnati, Ohio: Forward Movement Publications, 1973), p. 108.

[2]Joachim Jeremias, *The Lord's Prayer* (Philadelphia, Pa.: Fortress Press, 1964), p. 30.

[3]Joachim Jeremias, *Unknown Sayings of Jesus* (London: SPCK, 1957), p. 58.